A GUIDE TO TREASURE IN
PENNSYLVANIA

By Michael Paul Henson

*cover photo of Pennyslvania landscape
by Becky Sealand
submitted by Sealands Metal Detectors
Greensburg, Penna.*

TRUE TREASURE LIBRARY

Other books available from True Treasure Library —

- DIRECTORY OF BURIED OR SUNKEN TREASURES AND LOST MINES OF THE UNITED STATES
- TREASURE GUIDE TO NEBRASKA — KANSAS — NORTH DAKOTA — SOUTH DAKOTA
- A GUIDE TO TREASURE IN CALIFORNIA
- A GUIDE TO TREASURE IN TEXAS
- A GUIDE TO TREASURE IN ARKANSAS — LOUISIANA — MISSISSIPPI
- A GUIDE TO TREASURE IN ARIZONA
- A GUIDE TO TREASURE IN NEVADA
- A GUIDE TO TREASURE IN NEW MEXICO
- A GUIDE TO TREASURE IN MISOURI
- A GUIDE TO TREASURE IN UTAH
- A GUIDE TO TREASURE IN MONTANA AND WYOMING
- A GUIDE TO TREASURE IN ILLINOIS AND INDIANA
- A GUIDE TO TREASURE IN MICHIGAN AND OHIO
- A GUIDE TO TREASURE IN PENNSYLVANIA
- A GUIDE TO TREASURE IN VIRGINIA AND WEST VIRGINIA
- A GUIDE TO TREASURE IN KENTUCKY

FREE Treasure Reference Catalog.   Dealer Discounts available.

Copyright 1981
CARSON ENTERPRISES
P.O. Drawer 71, Deming N.M. 88031

ISBN 0-941620-14-X

All rights reserved. This book, or parts thereof, must not be reproduced in any form without permission.

INTRODUCTION

When an author attempts to compile the tremendous amount of research involved in a work of this scope and nature he has to use any source of material that he finds helpful. But because of the nature of treasure hunting he cannot hope to cover his subject completely. Others will know of locations that they will keep secret. No amount of persuasion will get information from these people because of distrust, superstition or fear of involving others.

Since the author has to rely on written history or oral traditions, he is subject to error. Sometimes his source of material for a location may be a story where no written historical facts can be found. Even history and geography are not always good guides to follow. Sometimes they do not agree on dates, places, nor in the manner in which events occured.

Because of erosion, road and dam building, strip mining of coal, streams having changed their courses, family traditions becoming exaggerated or different, authors giving their version of events or places, the basic facts concerning a treasure or relic site can become obscured with time.

A large part of the United States has no local written history, so the locations have to be researched by the author through oral traditions in the area where the incident occured.

No person can possible research all the locations in even one state without the help of others. Everywhere that man goes he leaves potential treasure in one form or another. Leads to treasure or relic sites can come in many forms, a legend, an old map, a rumor, newspaper clipping, sometimes only a whisper can lead to a profitable hunt.

There are different versions of all treasure stories not everyone will agree with the ones I have given. In this work I have listed the most widely accepted narratives and facts that time, research and history will allow. Every precaution has been taken to avoid errors and inaccuracies in this volume and it lays no claim to being all-inclusive on treasure or relic sites, because such an accomplishment covering this would be an impossibility.

Not all treasure is old, people still bury or hide their valuables because of distrust of banks or relatives and fear of a depression. Numerous people keep their savings at home. In hundreds of instances the person dies suddenly without revealing the location of their valuables.

The people that hid or buried their valuables most certainly meant to return and retrieve them at a more appropriate time. A time that in numerous instances, never came. A friend, members of the persons family, sometimes even a stranger, was given directions to a location, often by a dying or incoherent person. Due to the amount of time, distance and effort involved, the person with the directions was unable to find the hidden valuables. These people told someone else or wrote the information down and it was passed on to others. Thus a treasure story or legend was born, and like all stories, some were exaggerated. In some instances parts of the story were left out or had been forgotten.

An occasional mention is made in history books of a ship's sinking with a valuable cargo, a train or bank robbery, thus research into written history is the major key in obtaining hard historical facts. It is advisable to check all available sources of information before planning a treasure hunt. County and state records, old newspapers, historical societies, government census, senior citizens, surveyors and geologists reports are all invaluable aids in authenticating a treasure or relic sites. Regardless, to what extent the efforts may be in research, there will always be a doubt until the treasure is actually found. Remember, it is the perservering hunter that is the most successful.

I have followed a precedent of differentiating between metal detector sites and treasure locations.

Treasure locations - This is where a lost mine, or mines, lost, buried, sunken or hidden treasure has been documented or authenticated, as close to the truth as research and history will allow.

Metal detector sites - Relic hunting sites only. Ghost towns or near ghost are communities that have completely or almost completely disappeared. They are not included in the latest census and are not shown on current maps. Other locations are military or civilian trading posts, battlegrounds, old forts, cabin sites and camp grounds. A treasure hunter may find a few coin. or jewelry at these sites, but the primary reason for searching is to find historical relics.

Data on these locations can usually be obtained at the county seat of the county in which one intends to search To avoid problems in treasure and relic hunting in the state, permission should always be obtained and property rights respected. The searcher should leave the area exactly as it was found. If a proper approach is used, permission is usually granted. If each individual treasure hunter will follow these rules, others will have a better chance of gaining admittance to interesting and sometimes profitable locations.

HISTORY OF PENNSYLVANIA

The principal Indian tribes of early Pennsylvania were all of Algonquin stock. The Lemi-Lenape (Delaware) had several large villages. Shawnee, Minsi, Unami, Allegawes and Unalatka occupied the area.

Most of Pennsylvania's rivers were named for Indian tribes. Indian fighting was almost continual from about 1620 until the 1780's when most of the Indians were forced further west.

As the Indian was forced from his villages and hunting grounds he left ample evidence of his way of life for the archaeologist and treasure hunter. Implements of stone, flint, copper, clay and even gold and silver trinkets have been found by the thousands throughout Pennsylvania. The white man has added his lost treasures to those of the Indian. There are numerous authenticated and documented stories of lost, buried and sunken riches in Pennsylvania dating from 1616 to the present.

The first recorded visit by an European to this state was by Entienne Brule' in 1616. He was a Frenchman sent by Sieur Samuel de Champlain to explore the area south of the Great Lakes. The first settlements were made in 1643-81, by Swedish and Dutch traders in the lower valley of the Delaware River. The area was first named Penn's Woods in 1681, after William Penn. It was later changed to Pennsylvania.

During the Revolutionary War the state played a major part, with the Declaration of Independence being adopted at Philadelphia in 1776. This was also the seat of the Federal Government (except briefly in 1789-90) until 1800 when it was moved to Washington D.C.

During the War of 1812, over 50,000 men from Pennsylvania took part in the fighting. They helped win four major battles during this conflict. At the outbreak of the Mexican War in May 1846, four regiments volunteered from the Keystone State. During the Civil War, this state was invaded three times by the Confederates. The Battle of Gettysburg, fought July 1,2,&3, 1862, was the turning point of the war for southern invasion. Over 325,000 men from Pennsylvania fought during the Civil War, mainly for the Union.

For the treasure or relic hunter, the Keystone State offers almost countless sites of Indian villages, lumber camps, oil and coal "boom" towns (now ghost or near ghost towns), French, English and Colonial forts, trading posts, and missions, Indian, Civil and Revolutionary War battle sites, ship sinkings on Lake Erie and in the major rivers. For historical sites of the nation's history, Pennsylvania is ranked near the top in importance. These listings are in an alphabetical order of counties.

Commonwealth of Pennsylvania
Dept of Environmental Resources
P.O. Box 1467
Harrisburg, Penna. 17120

August 10, 1979
Refer to: RM-P-O

Mr. Michael Paul Henson
P.O. Box 980
Jeffersonville, Ind. 47130

Dear Mr Henson:

This is in response to your letter of August 6,1979, regarding the use of metal detectors in Pennsylvania State Parks.

There has been no change in our guidelines and policy as contained in our letter of June 23, 1978.

The reasonable use of metal detectors is permitted. Shovels, spades, garden trowels and other similar tools may NOT be used to dig into and to turn over ground areas that are covered by turf, vegetation, shrubs or trees. Permissible digging tools are screwdrivers, ice picks and other similar narrow prong devices. Metal detecting is not permitted where this activity would conflict with a facility in use, such as a bathing beach during busy summer days.

Items of a significant value that are recovered must be reported to the park office and to the Division of Escheats, Department of Revenue. A form to record the recovered items is available at the office.

Please notify the park office of your intentions prior to arrival.

I trust this provides the information sought. Thank you again for your interest and best wishes for a successful publication.

Sincerely,

(Signed)

R. E. Klingman, Chief
Program Services & Operations
   Division
Bureau of State Parks.

TREASURE SITES

ADAMS COUNTY - During June of 1863, when General Robert E. Lee pointed his grey coated legions north towards Pennsylvania, the state was in a panic. Confederate Generals Jubal Early (who had advanced to the city limits of Washington on one raid), J.E.B.Stewart and other top ranking Rebel officers were ordered to be the "eyes" of the advance by using fast moving calvary to reconnoiter the Union positions. One Confederate, Colonel E.V.White was ordered to break the railroad line at Hanover Junction.

The regiment set out on the Hanover Road. White planned to follow this route to the town of Hanover, 15 miles east of Gettysburg, and from there strike cross-country to Hanover Junction, ten miles further west.

On the road the column encountered a number of sutlers' wagons. These peddlers had followed the Union Army south and now found themselves in front of it as it moved north. They carried a wide variety of merchandise and made a good profit selling to the Union army. The money they carried made them a favorite target of Confederate raiders.

One sutler that White's troops encountered had his wagon loaded with jewelry. Much of it appeared to have been "borrowed" from plantation houses in Virginia that had been abandoned in the face of the Union's spring offensive.

Since there was too much for the men to carry and White did not want to slow his march by hauling the wagon, he ordered his troops to bury the jewelry near the road, hoping to return for it later. But the Battle of Gettysburg began the next day, and three days later the defeated Confederates began retreating to Virginia, leaving the jewelry buried along the Hanover Road.

ADAMS COUNTY - There is a longstanding legend of an Indian silver mine and cache of silver ingots being hidden in the area of Deep Run, Pennsylvania. This location is almost exactly on the state line of Pennsylvania and Maryland. However, most people believe the mine and cache to be within Adams County, Pennsylvania.The location and events covering this site were described in papers over 100 years ago.

The story goes that a German silversmith named Ahrwud was allowed to work a mine owned by local Indians. When Ahrwud's daughter betrayed the trust by stealing silver items from the mine, father, daughter and mine vanished.

The papers mention a stream and a large flat rock. Steps underground are mentioned, with the cryptic notation that they "should not be mistaken for Nature's opening."

The location is approximately one and one-half miles out of Union Mills, at the base of a hill. There could be some truth to this story as the mineral conditions are right for silver in this area.

ALLEGHENY COUNTY - This little known, 90 year old treasure site could very well pay for someone to check out. A small amount of currency was found, but this is believed to be only a part of what was hidden by the father, who dealt mostly in gold coins.

About four miles northeast of Hillsboro, Pennsylvania, John Crouch, called by his neighbors "a notorious miser", and his immediate family were murdered for money believed to be hidden either in or near the home. Speculation by different people, at the time, placed the amount at almost $350,000.

The Pittsburgh Dispatch of May 15, 1890, states that after the murders, Justice A.J.McCormich found $326.70, however the Pittsburgh Press newspaper rounds the figure to $250.00. Crouch's married daughter stated that there was over $3,000 in bills in the house and that her parents had many purses and that only one had been found, but she did not know how much gold her father had at home. A close relative denied that Crouch was a miser.

Three purses were taken from a man named West, the murderer.

It is noted that a will made out by Crouch in 1881 had left only $1,000 each to his children. The Pittsburgh Press states that Crouch was known to keep large amounts of money at his home, but does not state whether it was coin or currency, nor does it give the amount believed to still be hidden, although it does mention that it was considerable.

For those interested, this would be a good location for further research into the Crouch family and county records.

ALLEGHENY COUNTY - The warren was caught out on the shore at Pittsburgh in the spring of 1846 when the river fell, and was wrecked. She was a complete loss.

ALLEGHENY COUNTY - The Florence Bell, a packet that ran on both the Allegheny and Monongahela Rivers was cut down by ice at Creighton in January 1910.

ALLEGHENY COUNTY - The Ford City, a small towboat, burned at Pittsburgh on March 27, 1915, and was a complete loss.

ALLEGHENY COUNTY - The Forest and Pulaski collided about twenty miles above Pittsburgh on May 5, 1843. The Pulaski sank with quite a loss. She was raised and towed to Pittsburgh where she burned and sank on March 3, 1844. Salvage has never been reported.

ALLEGHENY COUNTY - The Liberty #2, a towboat, struck a pier of the St. Clair Street Bridge in Pittsburgh on June 19, 1855, sank and was a complete loss.

ALLEGHENY COUNTY - The Alice, a towboat, towed sand and gravel on the Allegheny River. Her boilers exploded near Glenfield and she sank. Eight men were killed.

ALLEGHENY COUNTY - During World War II, an Air Force bomber crashed into the Monongahela River near Hazelwood. Numerous people watched the plane crash, but no wreckage was ever discovered. The crash was a mystery that is still being talked about. The local theory is that the plane contained a large amount of money. How the money was retrieved (if it ever was) is unknown. This is almost certainly an overlooked treasure site.

ALLEGHENY COUNTY - The Cornplanter sank during February 1857, when she was caught in the ice below Brady's Bend on the Allegheny River.

ALLEGHENY COUNTY - The head of Turtle Creek, seven

miles southeast of Pittsburgh (Rankin, Pa. today) was the location in 1755, of probably the greatest upset victory in military history, and the reputed loss of between $15,000 and $25,000 in English gold coins. British Major General Edward Braddock had left Fort Cumberland, Maryland, with some 2,200 men and 20 pieces of artillery to attack the French fort of Duquesne at the forks of the Ohio River.

On June 9, 1755, near the ford on the Monongahela River, a few miles from the fort, Braddock's inexperienced troops were fired upon by French soldiers and their Indian allies. After suffering heavy losses, the British broke ranks and fled in panic. Braddock was wounded and died four days later. All of the expeditions supply wagons were captured except one, this wagon believed to have carried between $15,000 and $25,000 in English gold, expenses for the expedition plus Braddock's personal fortune. The driver, fearing capture by the French or Indians, is thought to have taken the road south along the Monongahela River to Fort Burd, later renamed Redstone Old Fort, in what is now Fayette Co.

Somewhere along this road he buried the gold and made his escape, later telling the story. (He could have told this story to cover his act of cowardice.) Official records are silent as to why the gold was never retrieved it is still a mystery. People have searched from Rankin, Pa., to Cumberland, Md., for this cache. There is no report that it has ever been found. (This is the accepted story of Braddock's lost gold today.)

I learned another version of this treasure story recently, first written in 1782, rewritten in 1853. Captains Dumas and deLigneris, with about fifty French regulars, pursued the remnants of Braddock's retreating army to the ford of the Monongahela River. The Frenchmen stopped here, then returned to the battle site to plunder. Charles Langlade, the half-breed Frenchman, who with Pontiac had led the Indians during the battle, gave a packet of military papers to the Commandant of Fort Duquesne, Pierre de Contrecaeur. Here are Langlade's exact words, "The men of Chief Pontiac found these in a chest on the field of battle. They wish to keep the chest but gave the papers to their chief who gave them to me." (These papers were English military plans that Braddock had been carrying.) This could indicate that the chest with the gold was found by the Indians and hidden or lost somewhere on, or near, the battlefield, since the Indians had no use for money.

Other theories have been pronounced concerning the missing money chest. One version is that the money could have been plundered by common soldiers of either side, another is that the Indians gained possession of it. According to one documented report, the chest apparently was left on the field of battle and fell into the hands of the French. The most popular expounded legend is that the money was hidden in one of the cannons and pushed over a ravine near Dunbar's Camp and remains to this day in some concealed crevice.

In the early 1960's, historian Edward G. Williams reported discovering an order among Braddock's papers sending the "money tumbril back to Fort Cumberland (formerly Wills Creek, now Cumberland, Maryland) a month before the defeat". However, receipt of the money was not documented. The mystery remains unsolved.

ARMSTRONG COUNTY - The Nellis Hudson ran on the Allegheny for several years. In 1913 ice sank her at Ford City.

BEAVER COUNTY - The area along the state line between East Liverpool, Ohio and Midland, Pennsylvania, was a wide open area for gamblers, bootleggers, and illegal stills during the 1890's. It has been estimated by knowledgeable people that over $1,000,000 came into the area each year through these illegal activities. The Dutch Zellner Gang ruled the region during this period, and there are several stories of hidden caches along the state line of Ohio and Pennsylvania. The library or county clerk at Aliquippi probably has records or newspaper clippings of this period that can help.

BEDFORD COUNTY - There is a legend, that dates to the late 1800's, of an old recluse burying over $100,000 on his farm in Oley Valley. The money was gold and silver coins. Check with the Historical Society at Reading for more information on this one.

BERKS COUNTY - For years the Doane Gang of Tories

had looted and terrorized the Pennsylvania countryside. Finally in 1777, farmers of Berks, Lancaster and Lebanon Counties revolted, surrounded the gang in Indian Gap near Wernersville and practically wiped them out. The gang's vast treasure, resulting from years of looting, is believed buried near the scene of their last stand.

BERKS COUNTY - The Historical Society of Reading can probably give data on this. It was almost a religious practice among the Dutch settlers to bury their money on their farms. There are several stories of family caches being made in this county. In several instances the money's owner died and did not reveal the location to anyone.

BRADFORD COUNTY - Spanish Hill or Carantouan is first mentioned in writing in 1614, on a Dutch map. In 1795, a Frenchman, Don de Rochefoucould-Lian-Court on a visit to the junction of the Chemung and Susquehanna Rivers wrote "four or five miles to the north I saw a mountain in the shape of a sugar loaf, upon which are to be found the remains of some entrenchments. The local inhabitants call them the Spanish Ramparts". In the 1840's a medal was found that was proven to have been made in 1550. Later, a Spanish sword, crucifix and a black, water-logged boat were found.

    Local tradition says the hill was used by Mound Builders, early French, Iroquoise Indians, and by three soldiers from a Swedish boat that was blown off course. All of this is theory. The evidence and most repeated stories say the ramparts were built by the Spanish about 1550. The early Indians told that men in iron hats came to the mountain to escape other men that were after them. The Indians called the mountain "Espana" or "Hispan" and said that none of their ancestors would visit the place. The men were supposed to have carried large chests full of round discs(coins) with them to the mountain and buried the chests in a cave. Both parties of Spanish were attacked by Indians and all were killed.

    In 1810, Alpheus Harris, a surveyor with a party of men sent to define the New York-Pennsylvania boundry line told of talking to the few Indians still living in the area. They would not approach Carantouan, and said the spirits of the dead men guarded the money chests.

In the 1820's, Joseph Smith (founder of the Morman Church) is known to have searched Carantouan for the money chests with a divining rod, without success. Others have searched unsuccessfully. As far as can be learned the chests of coins are still there.

BUCKS COUNTY - It is known that Indians obtained jasper near Durham Furnace. It was used for arrow and spear heads and jewelry. This location has never been found.

BUCKS COUNTY - A legend involves the Doanes in this county. The Doanes were a family of Tories who went outlaw during the Revolutionary War, attacking and robbing their Bucks County neighbors. A reward of $800 in gold was offered for the capture of this gang. Most members of the gang were captured, but without the stolen money. Some of the loot, believed to have been $19,000 in gold, was said to have been buried in a cave on the Delaware River near Point Pleasant. This cave had a small opening, easy to hide, and led to a larger cavern several yards from the entrance. Another location of buried loot was on Tohickon Creek. A third hoard of silver coins is believed buried on the Schuykill River outside colonial Philadelphia, along the rock wall of a potter's field grave yard.

BUCKS COUNTY - During the Revolutionary War, a British spy cached a large amount of gold coins near Bristol. The money was to have been used for the British cause during the war. Several stories differ on what happened to the spy. One is that he was hanged by the Pennsylvania Militia, another is that he was shot by Virginia patriots. The money was never reported found.

BUCKS COUNTY - A persistant legend in this county involves the mysterious Dr. John Bowman, who built a log cabin, sometime around 1700, in what is now Washington's Crossing State Park, on the Delaware River. Washington used Bowman's Hill as a lookout point prior to the battle of Trenton.

Dr. Bowman, some said, had been a member of Captain Kidd's crew, and had received a share of the pirates' booty. According to history, a Dr. John Bowman was captured and forced to sail with Captain William Kidd, as a ship's surgeon. About 1696, Bowman came up the Delaware River seeking a refuge. He had one more trip with Kidd, then returned to the cabin he had built on a hill overlooking the Delaware River. Kidd was caught and hanged in London. Dr. Bowman never went to sea again. He died in the cabin. His share of the booty during Kidd's pirate raids is believed buried near the cabin.

BUTLER COUNTY - About two miles southeast of the Old Stone Tavern, located on Route #8, is where a gang of counterfeiters and horse thieves had a hideout during the 1840's. A favorite practice of the outlaws was to waylay drovers and farmers, after they had spent a night at the tavern, and rob them. Stories of different caches in the area have been told for years.

CAMBRIA COUNTY - Millions of dollars were lost during the disastrous "Johnstown flood" of 1898. Most of this has not been recovered. One metal safe from a local bank held $50,000, and has never been found. Occasionally some objects are still being recovered by farmers while plowing along the river.

CARBON COUNTY - The outlaw, David Lewis, robbed people all over Pennsylvania and New York. Lewis claimed that in all his robberies he never killed a man. About 1815, Lewis teamed up with a killer named Conley. The two started such a series of robberies that armed men patrolled the roads every night in the Seven Mountains area of Central Pennsylvania. A reward of $600 was offered for the robbers, dead or alive. Eventually the two outlaws were cornered, Conley was killed and Lewis was taken to the jail in Bellefonte, with a shattered arm Lewis refused to have the arm amputated, gangrene set in and he died on July 13, 1820. Before his death, Lewis swore that he had buried a fortune in gold within sight of the jail.

CENTRE COUNTY - On Pine Creek is the site of Woodward Cave, one of the largest dry caverns in Pennsylvania. The cave is said to have been the hideout of a gang of robbers during the 1820's. Stories of hidden caches in and near the cave have been told in the area for years.

CENTRE COUNTY - A local legend tells that six barrels of gold were buried on the summit of Snowshoe Mountain near Wingate, at a tavern called Mountain House, in 1864. This money is supposed to have been taken from banks and hidden during the Civil War. In 1863, Pennsylvania was afraid that the Confederates would control the state. Thousands of banks closed, shipping their money east by wagon.

According to all available information the gold has never been found. In 1960, a man named Michael Furl claimed to have some knowledge of the hidden gold but was afraid to tell where it was because the government would take it. Furl had the information on the location from his parents. Furl died at Russville, Pa. in 1961.

CHESTER COUNTY - A cantankerous old fellow died in Chester County in a poor hut shortly after the Revolutionary War. He admitted that he had served the British as a spy during the war, but stated he had spent none of the gold coins received for his services. He had deposited the money in a crock and buried it near his hut.

As he lay dying, the old man asked a friend to dig up his crock of gold coins and spend the money for some worthy cause. Unfortunately, he passed away before being able to provide directions sufficient for retrieving the hoard. The county court clerk might possibly help locate where the old farm stood.

CHESTER COUNTY - Gold, nickel, copper and other minerals have been found here, also semiprecious stones such as garnet, beryl and amathust.

CHESTER COUNTY - South of Phoenixville are the Wheatley Mines. Before 1850, two veins of lead ore, containing silver were found. No mining has been done since the 1920's

CHESTER COUNTY - Near Brandywine is a place called

Hand's Pass. A cave in the mountain here is where the Fitzgerald gang had a hideout in the 1890's. They robbed several farmers and taverns in the area. Rumors of buried loot and money in or near this cave have circulated in the area for years.

CLARION COUNTY - The old Fox Mansion was built in the 1840's, by Joseph M. Fox. It sits on a high hillside and has been deserted for years, except for occasional visits by the family. The original owner owned 118,000 acres of land in the area and was considered wealthy. Local stories tell that he buried a considerable amount of money somewhere around the huge mansion. It is known that Fox, Sr. died just when the house was ready for occupancy. His grandson was also wealthy from income on oil properties he owned in the area. No report of this cache being found can be learned.

CLARION COUNTY - William Burdorf was a peculiar old man. He kept to himself, worked all his life and saved his money. It was common knowledge that he was quite rich when he died in November 1973. Burdorf's property was left to Dalton LeVier. LeVier hired a man named Jim Bish to take care of the property. Bish found a large amount of money buried beneath the barn's foundation. The money is being held in a special account at New Bethleham. The amount found is believed to be only part of the money hidden by Burdorf.

CLEARFIELD COUNTY - A lost lead and silver vein was discovered and lost again in the Stoneville area of this county. A trapper used raw lead and silver ore to make bullets when fighting Indians during the late 1700's. Some of this ore was found in his cabin after he died of natural causes. His cabin was located at the confluence of Little Clearfield Creek and Morgan Run. According to local stories, when he left the cabin to obtain lead he would be gone about one-half hour.

CLEARFIELD COUNTY - Along Clearfield Creek are the remains of an old farm called the Lambert Place. The owner, around 1914, was an old man that collected pennies. Many people in the area remember how the old man used to count a bushel basket full of pennies.

One afternoon he was seen to empty the basket into a large crock. The story is that he buried the pennies in a wooded area near his house. A bushel of pennies does not seem like a large treasure until you remember that all the pennies dated before 1914. The man died without revealing where the pennies were buried.

CLEARFIELD COUNTY - In 1946 a Meteorite fell during the summer, downing many trees and making a long furrow into the hillside of Missionary Ridge. The ridge is located at the junction of Doctor's Fork and Lick Run. The meteorite has not been recovered.

CLINTON COUNTY - For those interested in decoding or deciphering Indian symbols, this petroglyph offers a challenge. The following is taken from: "The Historical View of Clinton County, PA.," published in 1876.

In the year 1858, an engineer employed by the P & E Railroad found a very curious stone on which some characters were cut. The stone was flat, and was found under the ledge of rocks nearly opposite Keating Hotel.

On the rock were many images of various birds and animals. The most conspicuous carving was a rough draft of the West Branch of the Susquehanna River and Sinnemahoning Creek. The head of the creek was embellished with the likeness of an elk and the source of the river with the figure of a deer, seeming to point out that, on the creek elk were to be found, while the deer most abounded along the river.

CLINTON COUNTY - The Shamokin Path was a much traveled Indian trail. It followed the north shore of the Susquehanna River from present Sunbury to Great Island near LockHaven in Clinton County. It was used by the Delaware and Shawnee Indians on migration to the Ohio country before the French and Indian War. There are no known treasure sites along this trail but it would be a good road to search for Indian relics since it was used for years.

CLINTON COUNTY - Another ancient Indian trail worth searching was the Sinnemahoning Path. It connected the West Branch of the Susquehanna River with the upper Allegheny. It went from the Great Island at Lock Haven to the West Branch, then to the Sinnemahoning, then to Portage Creek and on to the Seneca Indian country. With the high price of Indian relics today, these two trails are worth investigating.

CLINTON COUNTY - Chadbert Joincaire was the Frenchman ordered to build the chain of forts from the Allegheny River to the Ohio River, then southwest to Illinois. This was just prior to the French and Indian War, which started in 1756. Joincaire used Indian labor and kept most of the money the French Government sent him. He is known to have buried caches at Fort Le Boeuf, Presque Isle, Vernango and Fort Machault. ($27,000 was found at Vernango about 1775; this had a tag with the initial J. stamped on the metal box, meaning it belonged to Joincaire).

The best place to search would be the old road Joincaire built from Warren to Coudersport. Anyone in Leidy can show you where the old road emerges from the woods in Clinton County. It is believed that Joincaire buried up to $500,000 at the different forts and along the roadway he built. Check with the Historical Society at Warren for information on the life of Joincaire.

CLINTON COUNTY - Somewhere on the grounds where Fort Horn stood is a document of priceless value. This was put into an iron box by the citizens of Pine Creek in July 1776. This document was a Declaration of Independence from the crown of England stating that the citizens of the settlement were free and independent. It was written probably within hours of the Declaration accepted by the Continental Congress in Philadelphia.

In 1778 the Six Nations with the help of the British all but wiped out the white settlement of Pine Creek. After 1779 when General Sullivan broke the power of the Six Nations, the settlers that remained returned to Pine Creek. Fort Horn had been burned and no trace of the town could be found.

Strange, that two documents of almost the same words could be written, although neither party knew that the other had been written. One is lost to history while the other became the greatest document in history. Our Declaration of Independence is secure, while the lucky person, if anyone ever does, that finds the Pine Creek document will have something priceless. This is an unusual treasure, but one worth the effort of checking out.

CLINTON COUNTY - About 1835, a man named Groves was visiting a man named Thomas Burns, on the West Branch of the Susquehanna River, two or three miles above Keating. While there he saw a party of Indians carrying knapsacks pass by going upstream. In a few days they returned and stopped at the Burns farm. Groves decided to see what the Indians had in the packs. During the evening meal he examined one of the bags and found it filled with high grade silver ore. After the Indians left, Groves backtracked them upstream to Birch Island Run, where the tracks went into the river. He could find no trace of the Indian silver mine. Groves searched (sporadically) but finally gave up. The area around Birch Island Run and Spruce Run is still wild, rugged country, but with modern methods of prospecting, this silver mine could be found.

COLUMBIA COUNTY - Northwest of Mill Grove is an old covered bridge across Roaring Creek. Local legend tells of a cache of gold coins buried here by a farmer that died before telling his family of the location.

COLUMBIA COUNTY - In June 1948, an airliner crashed into Mount Carmel. The story is that there was $250,000 aboard the plane. This money was in packets that were jettisoned just prior to the crash. None of the packets of money have been reported found. Wreckage of the plane was found over a wide area. Several reports put this crash in Northumberland County. But the County Clerk at Bloomsburg tells me that the incident happened in Columbia County.

    I quote this from the New York Times of June 1948: "Authorities were searching today for an air express package containing $250,000 in small bills believed jettisoned before the crash of a United Airlines DC-6 near here(Mt. Carmel), June 17th. A postal authority said the parcel of money weighed 240 pounds and contained bills in $1.00, $5.00 and $10.00 denominations".

COLUMBIA COUNTY - A band of Irishmen known as the Molly Maguires terrorized the coal fields in this county for years. The gang was finally broken up through the detective work of James McParlan. This gang had political connections clear up to the governor. There are several stories of hidden caches of gold made by members of this gang around Bloomsburg. The local library can furnish information on this notorious gang of outlaws.

DAUPHIN COUNTY - A group known as the "Paxton Boys" was organized from the Scotch-Irish settlements south of Harrisburg in 1769. Their raids on Indians were swift and merciless. They did not believe in leaving any Indian alive. There are stories that Lazarus Stewart, the leader, obtained large amounts of gold during the raids on Lancaster and that he buried several caches on his farm at Wyoming Valley.

DAUPHIN COUNTY - South of Devinshire Road and west of Nyes Road there is thought to be a vein of quartz that contains gold and silver. This story is old, dating back to pioneer days. At that time the ore wasn't worth the cost of mining. Could be worth checking out.

DELAWARE COUNTY - During the Revolutionary War, Hessians (Mercenary German Soldiers fighting for the British) are supposed to have dumped a cannon filled with gold coins into the Delaware River near Chester. This was done to keep the money from falling into the hands of the American Colonists. A check of the colonial army records might turn up something on this.

DELAWARE COUNTY - James Fitzpatrick and his partner Mordecia Daughtery were outlaws that preyed on Whigs in the region around Concordville during the 1789's. It is known that they robbed numerous people. It is believed that the two buried several caches of gold in the area before they were hanged.

DELAWARE COUNTY - Gold, nickel, copper and other minerals have been found here, also semiprecious stones such as garnet, beryl and amethyst.

ELK COUNTY - The Dent's Run treasure is said to be lost somewhere in the rugged, sparsely populated area where Elk and Cameron Counties meet. According to legend, a young Union Army lieutenant was commissioned in 1863 to transport a false bottomed wagon containing 26 gold bars weighing 50 pounds each from Wheeling, West Virginia to Washington.

Hoping to avoid Confederate troops, the lieutenant took a northern route. His plan was to bear northeast to the village of Driftwood on the Sinnemohoning River in Cameron, then build a raft and float down to the Susquehanna, on to Harrisburg, and eventually by land to Washington.

His party traveled through Pittsburgh, Clarion and Ridgeway, eventually arriving at Saint Marys in Elk Co. They left St. Marys for Driftwood one Saturday night in June, and were never seen again.

In August, the expedition's civilian guide wandered alone and hysterical into Lock Haven, about 40 miles southeast of Driftwood. He claimed all the other members of the expedition died in the snake-infested wilderness and the cargo was lost. Some believed him, but the Army was suspicious. The guide was questioned and kept under surveillance for years, and Pinkerton agents were called into the area. But the gold was never found.

ERIE COUNTY - Ten to fifteen miles northeast of Erie, the French frigate La Jean Florin sank in 1721. She is believed to have been carrying $500,000 in gold and silver bullion. A check of Coast Guard charts could help on this.

ERIE COUNTY - The Young Sion, carrying railroad iron and gold specie, sank about two miles off Walnut Creek, just east of Erie on June 12, 1881. Coast Guard charts give the latitude as 43-34.6 and longitude as 79-12.0.

ERIE COUNTY - The sidewheeler Atlantic sank on Aug. 19, 1852, in Lake Erie. The vessel was supposed to be carrying between $60,000 and $338,000 in gold in her safe. The strong box was recovered in June of 1856, containing about $36,000 of this amount. As far as can be determined the safe has never been salvaged and along with it the balance of the money remains hidden.

ERIE COUNTY - The John B. Lyon, a freighter, sank about four miles northeast of Girard on Sept. 11, 1900.

ERIE COUNTY - The barge, F.A. Georger, sank about four miles from Girard. She was carrying a load of iron worth about $100,000.

ERIE COUNTY - About one-half mile north of Erie is where the British Lion sank on October 27, 1891. She was carrying a general cargo.

ERIE COUNTY - The George M. Frost, a steamer, sank in Erie Harbor on September 2, 1879. She was valued at $100,000.

ERIE COUNTY - The Dundee, a schooner later converted into a barge, sank on September 11, 1900, near Girard, with a cargo of iron ore; estimated value was $50,000.

ERIE COUNTY - The Belle Mitchell, a schooner, foundered in a heavy southwest gale on October 14, 1886, and was a total loss. Total value of ship and cargo was put at $29,000.

ERIE COUNTY - Old records indicate that the sloop, Detroit, went to the bottom in 1797, three miles directly north of Erie. The water here ranges about 35 to 40 feet in depth. Cargo value is unknown, but she was carrying a load of military equipment.

ERIE COUNTY - The only clue to the "Spanish coin wreck" is the discovery near Erie of some Spanish pieces-of-eight minted in 1698. They were brought up by a sandsucker dredge recently. The captain noticed the coins lying on the top of the sand in one of the dredge hoppers shortly after he had to back his craft away from some underwater obstruction to avoid tearing his suction hose.

ERIE COUNTY - The Dean Richmond sank two miles north of Erie on August 19, 1893. She was carrying $141,000 in gold and $50,000 worth of zinc along with other cargo. She lies in about 130 feet of water.

ERIE COUNTY - There are several unidentified ships off the area of Erie. One such vessel is supposed to have been carrying a large amount of gold specie. A check of navigation charts kept by the Coast Guard might reveal information on this.

FAYETTE COUNTY - Anyone interested in cryptology should check the Indian picture rocks just off Route 201. These rocks are renouned as some of the best examples of picture writing in the country. Local legend says they tell of valuables hidden in the vicinity by Indians.

FAYETTE COUNTY - One of the long held legends around Uniontown concerns that of the Kirk Gang. The exploits of this band of outlaws are said to have ranged from Morgantown, W. Va. to the National Pike in Pennsylvania during the 1800's. A book called "The Rovers Den" was written about this gang in 1865. The story goes that in 1804 the band set up a hideout in Dulaney's Cave, (now Laurel Caverns) and buried a large amount of stolen money inside the cave. The outlaws were finally all killed but their reputed cache was never reported found.

FAYETTE COUNTY - Several years ago, 2,000 Indian Head pennies were stolen from a train near Uniontown by hi-jackers, who thought they were stealing two sacks of gold coins. In their disgust, they may have slung them off along the trail.

FAYETTE COUNTY - There is supposed to be a fabulous treasure of silver bars hidden in a cave near Uniontown. The amount of silver bars are supposed to weigh a staggering one hundred fifteen tons.
   There are two stories as to how the loot got where it is. One says it was shipped by ox cart from Buffalo, New York, to prevent it from falling into the hands of the British during the War of 1812. The other story tells that it was hi-jacked from a train in 1865, during the Civil War.

FRANKLIN COUNTY - During the 1840's, a farmer named Johnson lived in York County Pennsylvania. He had a contract with the U.S. Army to raise horses. When a string became old enough to sell he would deliver them to Pittsburgh and receive payment.
   On one trip, as he was returning home, he stopped in

Bedford, Pennsylvania, where he started drinking and gambling. Later he was accused of card cheating and badly beaten by the four men with whom he was gambling. Johnson died soon after and his body was sent home to his wife, minus his money.

A short time later, one of the gamblers bragged about the beating of Johnson in Dillsburg, Penna. The widow heard about it and went looking for the gamblers. By the time she got to Shippensburg, she had killed three of the men that had beaten her husband and had taken their money.

She traveled northwest and camped at a place that was later called Widow Springs. The next morning she was found dead. It is believed the fourth man learned she was after him and killed her during the night. Several coins have been found in the area over the years, but the treasure of Widow Springs is still missing.

FOREST COUNTY - It is almost a certainty that an Indian silver mine exists near Tionesta. First, and perhaps foremost as to the proof of the existence of such mineral wealth can be found on Tract Number 2827 in what was once known as Pinegrove Township. There are evidences of ditches and trenches extending for hundreds of yards, with branches connecting to each parallel. Everything indicates the terrain was once worked systematically and extensively.

Years after the Treaty of Frot Stanwix, in which the Six Nations ceded all of northern Pennsylvania to the United States in consideration of the paltry sum of $4,000, small bands of Senecas would return to the Tionesta region.

In 1866, a Frenchman from the midwest visited the Tionesta region in search of silver. He finally gave up his search and left Tionesta mysteriously. It is not known whether he found anything, but there is reason to believe he did.

In 1845, a lone redman from Wisconsin, of Seneca ancestry visited the tiny village. Well learned in the white man's ways, he explained that he had learned from unerring traditions of elders of the few Senecas who fled west following the route of crafty Little Turtle at Fallen Timbers in 1794, that silver was to be found in Tionesta valley. Whatever the Indian found, he kept to himself, nor did he reveal the source of the fabled lead and silver to any of his white brothers.

In 1878, the "Forest Press", the publication of the wilderness wrote,"it is well known to early settlers that a white man on friendly terms with the Senecas, was shown the mines. He was blindfolded before he was taken to the grounds, as a precaution. He saw the mineral which he was positive was silver".

The writer of the day might have been very successful as a modern treasure hunter. He wrote: "What are the evidences that such minerals as alluded to ever exist within our borders? The first is tradition. Tradition has been well defined by one writer as 'unwritten history' descending from oral accounts from age to age. Therefore if a history was current throughout the past, some foundations exist, or the promulgators of the error would fall under the ban of being imposters, and if the same item was alluded to by a nation noted for it's veracity, it was a matter easily detected and proved."

The writer of another era further states,"The theory that valuable lead and silver mines exist in Forest County, is based on the fact that this was the last region to be vacated by the red man, and the fact that small groups of them returned almost on an annual basis."

No known visits by Indians have been made in recent years.

FULTON COUNTY - According to local stories, there is a lost Indian silver mine located in the vicinity of McConnellsburg. During the last Indian Wars, 1780-1790's Indians are supposed to have obtained silver ore that they traded to white settlers. Could pay to check this out since silver has been found in Pennsylvania.

HUNTINGDON COUNTY - Fresh water pearls have been found in the Aughwick River, which crosses the entire county.

JUNIATA COUNTY - Fresh water pearls have been found in the mud banks of the Juniata River which flows through this county.

LACKAWANNA COUNTY - A $70,000 payroll, buried by three robbers who derailed the train carrying it and killed the engineer, is still hidden. They were caught later and hung without divulging the location. As close as can be determined, the treasure lies somewhere in Warrior Gap, located just slightly north of Interstate 81.

LACKAWANNA COUNTY - In 1927, a pay car for the coal mines was blown up by two men. A large charge was used and the car and occupants were blown apart. More than $27,000 was spread over an area of 700 feet. Almost all of the greenbacks were recovered, however, $6,000 in coin still lies scattered in that particular section of woods located near Wilkes Barre, in the vicinity of Espe Gap.

LACKAWANNA COUNTY - During the late 1920's, Jake Swanson lived on Bell Mountain near Eynon. Old Jake collected garbage from the city of Scranton to feed his hogs. He never went anywhere and spent only what money he had to. Because of a dispute among bank officials in the North End Bank in Scranton, old Jake withdrew all his money. A clerk swore that old Jake put over half an oil drum full of silver dollars on his wagon and took it to his shack on Bell Mountain. Jake returned and got another half a drum full. This nearly broke the bank. When Jake died a few years later, only three silver dollars were on his body. The old farm is overgrown now and is located near the top of Bell Mountain. Somewhere in the area is a 55 gallon oil drum filled with silver dollars.

LANCASTER COUNTY - Near Christiana is where, prior to the Civil War, several farms were located that were hidding places for runaway Negro slaves. They were held here until they could be sent to Canada. Stories of slave hunters tracking slaves to this area and recapturing them have been told in the area for years. Locations of money hidden by these slaves to prevent the hunters from taking it are believed to be on several of these farms.

LANCASTER COUNTY - A good location to do local research on highwaymen that operated during the 1740's, is around Lancaster. These robbers infested the roads, making travel dangerous. No known organized gangs operated at this time, but numerous individuals carried on a profitable trade in whole sale robbery in the area. Taverns and farmers were robbed, livestock stolen and homes burned.

LANCASTER COUNTY - As early as 1708, iron copper and nickel mines were being worked by settlers from Maryland, in this county. The locations of several mines that were worked between 1708 and 1730 were lost. The Historical Society at Lancaster could have information on these early mines.

LEBANON COUNTY - Check the streams in this county as most of the gold found in Pennsylvania has been found here, produced from the Cornwall iron mine. Magnetic ore was discovered in the 1740's, yielding 32% sulphur, 25% copper and some gold and silver.

LEHIGH COUNTY - Near Vera Cruz are the Indian Jasper quarries. Articles made of this jasper were carried by the Indians as far away as England.

LEHIGH COUNTY - A cache of gold coins of an undetermined amount is supposed to be buried on a farm between Emmans and Macungie. Several people have searched the farm which is called Haunted House. About twenty-five years ago the story was circulated in the area that the treasure had been found, but it was learned later to be a hoax. As far as can be learned, the money, hidden by a farmer, is still there.

LUZERNE COUNTY - In 1788, a gang of outlaws operated near Wilkes Barre at a place called the "Coalbeds". They raided farms and robbed travelers in the area. They were finally driven away by the Pennsylvania militia. Their hideout was four log cabins near the Susquehanna River. Legends of buried gold at their hideout by this gang still circulate in this area.

LUZERNE COUNT - About four miles from Wilkes Barre, on Laurel Run Creek, there is supposed to be a $12,000 lumber company payroll hidden in a tin box. This was being carried on the railroad by a contractor for the lumber company. The money was stolen by a bandit named Michale Rizzalo and two other men in 1888. Rizzalo was arrested in 1889. He named as his accomplices, Guiseppe Benevino and Vincent Valalli. While Rizzalo was in jail his two partners escaped to Italy. The two were caught later, they swore that Rizzalo had hidden most of the $12,000. Rizzalo was executed June 25th, 1889, for the murder of two guards during the robbery. By checking the records of railroad and contractors that operated in the area at that time, this could prove profitable.

McKEAN COUNTY - There is a treasure legend, recent in origin, that is an excellent treasure lead. It's said that sometime around 1890, a robber buried his loot under the Kinsue Bridge, a local landmark. The bridge is located northeast of Mt. Jewett. The man robbed a bank in Emporium, Cameron County, and made off with $60,000. It is believed he also robbed a general store near Clermont in McKean County. No one knows for sure. The man wandered into Hazel Hurst, sick and delirious - and without the money. Just before he died he said he buried the money under a flat rock within sight of the Kinzue Bridge. Crews sent out by the railroad, as well as local fortune seekers, looked for the money, supposedly buried in glass jars, but it was never reported found.

MERCER COUNTY - It could pay to check with the county clerk in New Castle for the locations of old truck stops and saloons that were in operation during prohibition. Youngstown, Ohio, just across the state line was a favorite hangout and stop over for whiskey runners and bootlegeers on their way south from Cleveland and Chicago. Several of these nefarious characters frequented New Castle to gamble and get drunk. Several stories of caches being buried in the area have been told.

McKEAN COUNTY - Of all the counterfeiters that have operated in Pennsylvania during the last 300 years, Cyrus Cole was perhaps the smartest and certainly the longest in this nefarious occupation.
    No one can be certain how many dies for the making of bogus silver and gold coins remain hidden in the marshlands adjoining the village of Eldred. Furthermore, money taken in exchange for the counterfeit coins, most feel, was cached somewhere in the wasteland.
    The man behind all of this was a simple man who was regarded as the town character of the little village. Cyrus "Cy" Cole wouldn't hurt a flea. An "odd ball",

Cole spent most of his time in the marshland north of the village, where he ran a trapline for muskrat and mink. While Cy seemed to know his way around the bog, he proved to be the world's worst trapper, seldom bringing in more than a 'rat or two at a time. Fifty cents a hide was all the fur dealers paid in 1910.

He supplemented his supposedly meager income by picking berries which he sold house to house, or by running a few errands. Still Cy at times displayed some signs of affluence, and many felt that he had an income from oil interests. McKean county was the first billion dollar petroleum field, and there were a number of eccentric people of supposed wealth in the area. Many deduced that Cole had made it 'big' but preferred to live the life of a recluse.

Meanwhile in Washington, the Secret Service had been baffled by the passing of phony half dollars and five dollar gold pieces. The similarity to the genuine was so striking as to confound experts at first glance. The east had been flooded with the replicas, and many had mysteriously appeared in Canada. For months the best inspectors in the service had tracked down leads, only to learn of a new outbreak of worthless coin passing in another state. It was a baffling case, and obviously the ring was well organized, and the expertise of the engraver was superb.

In the fall of 1912, Inspector Nye of the Pittsburgh office received an anonymous letter, from Eldred, Pennsylvania. The writer described the operations of a gang of counterfeiters operating in the village, headed by a crafty operator named Cryus Cole. The informer went so far as to claim that Cole had dies and molds hidden in compartments beneath his windows

An agent was sent to the tiny Allegheny River village. There had been rumors that the recluse was far better off financially than most believed, and some had even remarked as to his cunning and guile. There were even a few who feared the man. The result was a warrant was obtained, and a routine search was made of Cole's little home.

Cole was absolutely inscrutable, when he was given a clean bill of health. Suddenly the visiting officer recalled that the molds were secreted beneath the windows. One window after another revealed nothing but a solid frame, and crystal clear Hazelhurst Plate Glass. Finally checking beneath one window, Nye removed a slide that moved on a track, like the cover on a school child's pencil box. Out tumbled a mold, obviously meant for making coins. There were also a few beautifully drawn detailed sketches. When confronted with the evidence, Cole had not the slightest idea of how the objects had gotten there. He insisted it was a plant, and later developments indicated perhaps it was.

Cole was arrested and charged with possession of equipment which could be used to duplicate United States coins. He was taken to Warren, Pennsylvania, to await a hearing before a United States Judge in Erie. In the meantime, a number of agents combed the swamp looking for the Cole 'mint'. Nothing was ever found.

Detailed investigation prior to the trial divulged that Cole had a habit of duplicating the work of the Philadelphia mint and the Bureau of Printing and Engraving. The amiable 'muskrat' trapper had been in frequent trouble, but Cole was crafty and managed always to slip out of the clutches of the law.

Inspectors believed that he passed rolls of bogus gold pieces just to demonstrate to his many agents that the risk was slight. The deduction was that the 'seedy trapper', mass produced his wares in the swamp, where he could be almost certain of freedom from detection. His dies and molds were engraved at home, by the light of the midnight oil. The baser metals which had to be smelted were picked up from neighboring junk yards. The gold and silver gilt paint, Cole procured from a wholesaler in Buffalo. Cole sole his coins to 'passers' on a discount, or commission basis for the 'big dealers'. He took few risks. His visitors were 'passers' and 'dealers'.

The real money, Cole received in the exchange, which had to be substantial, was not deposited in any of the area's banks, nor any other for that matter.

Without question, one of Cole's 'agents' blew the whistle on him. In 1913, agents combed the swamp looking for Cole's 'money factory' but found nothing. Nor was any cache of genuine wealth found. Yet it is a safe bet that the heavy game bag that Cole often carried to the marsh, contained not traps, but money.

Dies, molds, and genuine gold and silver coins are

buried somewhere in the swamp, probably on one of the higher points. Cole was not simple enough to set up shop in the areas where a sudden flash flood would carry off his ill gotten gains. Since he frequently visited the mountain east of the village, some of the loot may be buried in that section among the oil pumping jacks and abandoned pumper's shacks.

Neither Cole not the agents ever carried a dime out of Eldred. Cole's travels were limited to neighboring Larabee and Port Allegany. The evidence that would have sent Cole 'up the river' for a long stretch, plus hundreds of bogus and genuine coins remain hidden near the village.

MIFFLIN COUNTY - This story of $650,000 worth of pennies takes some explaining, but it is true. Since a story of this nature must have made big news, I checked two newspapers, the "Philadelphia Ledger" of Philadelphia and "The Sentinel" of Lewistown, Pennsylvania, and here briefly are their reports.

On December 1, 1909, the Pittsburgh Express train, on its way from Washington, D.C., to Pittsburgh, Pennsylvania, had just passed Mifflin and entered the "narrows" near Lewistown. A lone bandit (later identified as James Lawler, one of the two Lawler brothers, the other named John, notorious criminals of the area) with a pistol in each hand and sticks of dynamite in his coat pockets, disrupted the passenger train by setting off some of the explosives and shaking the train.

The engineer stopped the train and the lone bandit, who had a burlap bag mask with two holes for eyes, confronted the engineer and conductor, forcing them to lead him to the express car. After entering the express car the bandit called for more efficiency from the trainmen because of their slowness in reaction to his demands. He fired several shots and wounded the conductor, Poffenberger, in the hand. The bandit forced the conductor, fireman and another man to carry bags of loot several hundred yards up a mountain bordering the tracks, then ordered them to go back down to the train while he made his getaway.

One bag contained $5,049 in gold, two bags contained Lincoln pennies, $100.00 in each bag, the first ever minted. One small bag contained $100.00 worth of silver dollars and a small pouch contained $10.00 in silver dollars.

On arrival at the scene a few hours later, Pinkerton Agency detectives and other railroad employees, plus local law officials, found a trail of money up the mountainside. First was found the bag of gold, $5,049, then farther up was found another bag, then the other bags. The bags of pennies had been slit. All the money was found with the exception of $65.00 .

My evaluation of this is, the bags of pennies would have weighed about 86 pounds, the gold about 16 pounds and the other bags much less. The robber probably fumbled around with all the bags and after much trouble just cast away the smallest bags, retaining the heaviest ones. After more trouble he probably decided to open a bag and fill his pockets and stash the rest.

When he discovered he had only pennies, he heaved these bags away then could not find the first one containing the gold due to darkness. He probably had wasted a lot of time struggling with his 175 pounds of supposedly treasure before his discovery. He actually got away with nothing. The robber was never caught and it is believed to have died in the mountains west of Lewistown. His brother, John was later hanged in West Virginia.

In 1909, railroad and local officials were not concerned with a lost bag of pennies when they had just recvered the rest of the robbery money. When the robber slit the bags and threw the pennies away in 1909, they were worth $65.00, but if the coins were in mint condition and are 1909 VDB-S, their estimated value today would be well over half a million dollars.

In December of 1954, three deer hunters, Johnny and Albert Dubendorf, with a friend, Charles Bell, were returning home from a hunt about a half-mile east of Hawstone. Bell discovered several pennies. The three men began digging and uncovered 3700-1909 pennies. This had to be part of the $65.00 that Lawler threw away

Since then there have been no reports of anything else being found. This would be a good place to search, because somewhere in the area where the hunters struck their bonanza, there are still 2800 pennies, worth a minimum of $11,000 on today's market, waiting for lucky treasure hunters.

McKEAN COUNTY - A million and a half dollars worth of silver bars are believed buried near Silvermine Run, about five miles west of Gardeau by a Captain Blackbeard (not the pirate). He had a commission from the British admiralty to raise the hulk of a Spanish treasure ship which had been wrecked off the Bahamas in 1680. He successfully salvaged the vessel, landing the wreck at Baltimore, where a warship was scheduled to tow it and the loot it contained to London.

But, on the eve of the War of 1812, in June of that year, Captain Blackbeard met an acquaintance, Peter Abelard Karthaus, of the privateer Comet, on the Baltimore docks. Karthaus was aware that Captain Blackbeard had successfully brought to the Maryland city the Spanish galleon with its $1,500,000 worth of silver bars.

Possibly the fear that Karthaus might pirate the find plus the fact that, with war iminent, the British had put into effect a blockade of the Eastern coast, caused Captain Blackbeard to decide that his silver treasure should be transported overland to safety in Canada.

He started to haul his silver bars across Pennsylvania with a convoy consisting of six wagons, each of which was drawn by six oxen. When the war actually started, the convoy was in McKean County, and here news came to Captain Blackbeard that Niagara had been blockaded, closing off his intended route of escape. He then buried his treasure somewhere near Silvermine Run.

Soon after it was hidden, Captain Blackbeard sent a Colonel Noah Parker to the treasure site. Here Colonel Parker kept intruders away until his death many years later, by which time the hiding place was forgotten, and the story surrounding it became a vague legend in the community,

Colonel Parker's castle and his mausoleum with its Masonic emblem as a weathervane can still be seen from Pennsylvania Railroad trains traveling from Harrisburg to Buffalo.

MIFFLIN COUNTY - Fresh water pearls have been found in the mud banks of the Juniata River.

MIFFLIN COUNTY - A treasure of currency known as

the Fracker Treasure is buried in the vicinity of Lewistown. Since this happened not too many years ago, local newspapers could tell the whole story.

MONROE COUNTY - Hidden somewhere within the Delaware Water Gap lies a copper strong box filled with the payroll for a railroad construction gang. Buried there by the paymaster when he became ill and died soon after from a heart attack. The key to this chest was recovered near the site where he beached his canoe but the chest has never been found.

MONTGOMERY COUNTY - The Black Horse Tavern, located on the road from Philadelphia to Valley Forge was a notorious hangout for outlaws and Tories during the 1770's. Travelers were poisoned then robbed. There are several stories of buried money and silver plate around the tavern.

NORTHAMPTON COUNTY - Indians used jasper for arrow and spear heads. It was mined in the southwestern part of this county. It could pay to search for any of the mines, with the price of jewelry what it is today.

NORTHAMPTON COUNTY - Near Raubville, on a place called Hexicoff Hill, there is supposed to be a lost jasper mine known as the Bear Rock Jasper Mine. The County clerk tells me by letter that there is no known location of Bear Rock, there is a rock called Elephant Rock now in the area. There is evidence still being found where Indians mined Jasper, using it for arrow and spear heads and jewelry.

NORTHUMBERLAND COUNTY - About 1800 a man named James Silverwood claimed a group of seven islands in the Susquehanna River. He called himself "Master of the Seven Islands". He was considered wealthy for the time and was supposed to have kept a large amount of money on one of the islands where he lived. Local stories say that before he died, he buried the gold near his home, and never told anyone where it was.

NORTHUMBERLAND COUNTY - John Mason was known as

the "Hermit of Blue Hill". He built a two story octagonal house on top of this hill and lived alone. The only time he left his home was to obtain supplies at Sunbury or Northumberland. There are stories of this old bachelor burying money somewhere around his home. He had a large library consisting of hundreds of rare old books and was always known to have plenty of money. He was buried behind the old house where he lived. He died alone and it was several days before his body was found.

NORTHUMBERLAND COUNTY - One of the few women counterfeiters to ever operate in Pennsylvania was Ann Carson. She and two companions also robbed cattle drovers. At one time she had an elaborate scheme to kidnap the governor's son and exchange him for her lover, Lieutenant Richard Smith. The scheme failed and Smith was hanged. The money she obtained in her outlaw career is believed hidden somewhere near her home.

She often masqueraded as a Quakeress and passed a considerable amount of imitation money. She was finally caught and sent to prison where she died in April 1824.

PERRY COUNTY - Fresh water pearls have been found along the banks of the Juniata River, which flows through this county.

PHILADELPHIA COUNTY - The British battle ships Augusta and Merlin were sunk in the Delaware River during October 1777, as they were attacking Fort Mudd and Fort Mercer, on either side of the Delaware River at the edge of Philadelphia. Both ships burned and sank during the attack. The Augusta's remains were visible for many years. Rumors that their cargo included a considerable treasure have been circulating for years.

PIKE COUNTY - Near where Port Jarvis was located where Daniel Skinner, one of the first timbermen in Pennsylvania, lived in the 1760's. He and his crews would raft 80 foot logs down the Delaware River to Philadelphia where they were sold for gold. Skinner would accept nothing else. The logs were to be used for ship masts. Local stories say that Skinner buried part of his huge earnings on his farm.

PIKE COUNTY - An Indian treasure that almost certainly has not been found is hidden in the valley of Wallenpaupack, near Hawley, Pennsylvania, on the Pike-Wayne county line. The cache consists of jewels, beads, gold and silver ornaments, rawhide bags of "stone" money and a large variety of Indian artifacts, once the property of the proud and peaceful Paupacken Indians, a branch of the Delawares. It was concealed by the tribal cheif to keep it from falling into the hands of hostile New York warriors who eventually drove the Paupacken from the valley.

The last known of the Paupacken tribe, the lovely princess Nemanie, met a white settler one day. She explained in broken English and sign language that all her people were gone. Her husband, Chief Paupackan, was gone too, for he had been killed. "Today we are at the end, those few remaining have gathered our dead, buried our treasures and fled into the deepest of forests. Now I to go to join Paupacken in the land of hereafter." With these words she leaped into the rushing waters of the creek. Thus the peaceful Paupacken Indians disappeared among the pine trees forever.

The Wallenpaupack Valley lies within the Pocono Mountains of Pennsylvania and is a natural wonderland. The most probable spot to search for this cache lies just off Route 507, between the villages of Paupack and Tafton. To reach the area from the east, take Interstate 84 or Route 6, from Interstate 84 take Route 507 North to Paupack. From Route 6 take 507 south. North and South use anyhighway to Interstate 80 or take Route 81 north and south to Interstate 80. This would be a good site to check out.

PIKE COUNTY - Very few people even know of this obscure treasure cave or mine located at Shohola Glen, Pennsylvania. According to the tale, the cave could be entered from some hidden cranny in the ravine. Another entrance was reported to be in Panther Brook Glen, a mile away. An Indian trail running parallel with the Delaware River and crossing the Shohola, was visible for many years.

From time to time an Indian from an eastern reservation was known to have visited the glen, lending credence to the belief that the tribesman knew of the treasure or mine and drew upon it when necessary. In addition, it was said that Indians of the region fought with silver-headed arrows and silver bullets. Be that as it may, it was reported that a settler named Helm had long ago befriended an Indian Chief in this area. For some reason the chief wished to impress Helm by showing him this mysterious cave.

However, when the two men reached Shohola Glen, the thief blindfolded Helm for the remainder of the journey. Once in the cavern, the Indian removed the blindfold. There, to Helm's amazement, piled about the floor, were mounds of crude silver. Although they had only a torch for a light, Helm could see that he was gazing at an immense fortune. Covering Helm's eyes again, the chief led him from the cave by way of the exit to Panther Brook Glen.

Helm spent the rest of his life searching for this cave, and even married a squaw, hoping to gain the confidence of the tribe. However, she never dared to tell him until she was on her deathbed. Then her attempt to describe the cave's location was confused in semi-conscious rambling, leaving her husband with no concrete information. Helm, too, went to his grave a few years later without having found the treasure.

POTTER COUNTY - There are thousands of gold and silver coins, rings, lockets, bracelets and other personal jewelry, plus thousands of antiques, waiting to be found on an eight or nine mile stretch of flatlands below Austin. September 30, 1911, a dam, 534 feet across and 43 feet high broke and an estimated 500,000,000 gallons of water rushed down on the town of Austin. The entire length of Freeman Valley was washed clean. Damage was estimated at ofer $5,000,000. Eighty bodies were found. Today Austin has only about 600 people, in 1911 there were at least 3,000. The value of articles lost along the path of this indirect man-made flood could reach into the thousands. Several old-timers in the area can still remember that terrible day and can point out landmarks and the flood's path. This could be a profitable stretch of land for a treasure hunter to investigate.

POTTER COUNTY - This is a combination of three treasure locations, all in the same area. The stream, Thunder Run, drains into Johnson Brook in Pike Township, near Galeton, Pennsylvania. It got it's name from the continuous rumbling roar, like distant thunder, that comes out of the hill near its head. The tumbling and churning of water inside the hill is what causes the noise. The noise is loudest and most active in the spring when the rainfall is greatest. Part of this stream is above ground, in other places it is deep within the earth.

There is a story of a "diamond mine" in Johnson Brook. Several people claim that on Thunder Run, anyone willing to dig, can pick jewels out of the dirt that look like real diamonds, but they are of no great value. However, these imperfect stones could indicate a deposit or a "pipe" that certainly needs to be investigated further.

During the period before the Civil War, there was a gang of horse thieves who had hide-outs in several different places in the county. One of these was in Sandstone Hollow, this is the first small stream that drains into Pine Creek west of Galeton, another was in Thunder Run. The thieves would hide the horses in one of the numerous caves in the area until the lawmen stopped searching for them. There was a cave (or tunnel) connection between these two streams that allowed the outlawns to outwit any posse that was chasing them.

One member of the gang was such a good painter that he could change the color of a horses' hair so that it could not be identified until the hair was shed. Stories of hidden caches being made by these thieves have circulated in the area for years.

About 105 years ago, a young boy names Charlie Smith, with a companion, decided to explore the small caves along the rocks in Sandstone Hollow. After a few hours in one cave, they came to a wide fault, which in places had large rooms and high ceilings. They needed no lamps because light filtered down from cracks in the fault.

They walked and crawled for over half a mile before they came out on Thunder Run, proving that the two streams were connected by a cave system. On their way through this natural tunnel the two boys saw numerous weapons and tools made by Indians from flint and bone. The two never told their parents about their cave exploring trip until they were grown, for fear of being punished by their parents for doing such a dangerous thing. Any interested spelunker would do well do visit Sandstone Hollow.

POTTER COUNTY - This location of buried coins is almost unheard of outside the little town of Roulette, Pennsylvania.

Dabole Hare came to Roulette (spelled Roulet at that time) in 1830 and settled on a little farm in Halfway Hollow, which he had purchased from John Keating, once an officer in the service of Louis XVI. Halfway Hollow is the first road off present day Sartwell Creek Road just a few miles from the village which had no association with a French gambling game. Hare was sixty years old when he came to the little village on the banks of the upper Allegheny River. Obviously affluent, Hare was also frugal in his spending. Never trusting banks and having an impassioned hatred toward suggestions for investment of his wealth, Hare made himself unpopular in Roulette.

The aged man would never spend a gold coin, although he showed a marked preference for being paid in that manner, by all who owed him--which was quite a list. Depositing his coins in large milk cans, which he kept hidden in the fields near the little home, Hare finally got to the point where he could not remember himself where all the hiding places were.

On Sunday afternoon, April 7, 1850, the octagenarian thought he would take a little walk along the river and perhaps gather a few leeks, maybe even drown a few worms. Along with that he would visit his son-in-law, George Lehman, on the south shore of the historic flow. To cross to the opposite side, Hare had to walk a rickety log footbridge. He never made it to the other side.

Late in the afternoon the entire village turned out to search for the aged man. Checking the bridge, the party saw that the railing had collapsed, dumping the 80 year-old man into the swollen waters. His cane lay on the bridge. The deduction was that he had been swept down the stream toward Port Allegheny and had been drowned.

Dabole's body was later found some distance downstream. Several searches were made for his caches, but as far as can be learned, none of them have ever been found.

POTTER COUNTY - Old French records tell that in 1616-1618, when Etienne Brule (the first white man to visit Pennsylvania) and his men searched for a silver mine known to the Indians, that they looked on Hammersley's Fork of Kettle Creek. To confirm this legend, a vein of ore that, when assayed, showed traces of lead and silver, was found in 1880. There is a deep shaft still visible and nearby is parts of an old smelter. This site could pay off with more investigating.

POTTER COUNTY - Most of the early settlers in Pennsylvania were law abiding citizens but the logging era of the 1850's brought all kinds of rough lumberjacks into the state. One such man was Mark McCoy. He would pretend to work in the woods during the day but at night he was a highwayman. On numerous occasions he robbed people along the Turnpike Road in Stewartson Township. He always carried two pistols and somehow managed never to be caught. McCoy once robbed five constables that were trying to catch him.

One day in about 1853, a young attorney from Smithport, Pennsylvania, was on his way to WIlliamsport with a large sum of money. Refusing to stop when McCoy told him to, he was shot in the back and died two hours later. McCoy, realizing that he had to get away, went to his girlfriend's home where he caught her with another man. McCoy killed them both. He then returned to the Turnpike Road, climbed a tree and hanged himself. His body was found the next day by the sheriff and a posse. All they found on the corpse was $200 in gold and silver coins. What happened to the hundreds of dollars McCoy was known to have obtained in his numerous robberies? The money was not found by the authorities. This would be a very good site for further research.

POTTER COUNTY - The only workable gold mine in Pennsylvania is located south of Coudersport. Sometime during the 1870's, a disabled Union Army veteran named Merrick Jackson, found an unusual outcropping of sandstone near his home. He knocked off several pieces of the rock after he noticed the glint of something yellow. At home he broke the samples apart then decided to have them assayed at Williamsport.

He was shocked to learn that the samples were gold bearing rock worth $16.00 per ton. Jackson and several other men crushed the stone and washed the accumulated sand, recovering a few grains of gold. After a few months they realized that the mine would not pay with such primitive methods so they stopped working it.

The crude mine was taken over by a mining company in 1938, but the high cost of mining and extraction of the small amounts of gold caused the attempt to fail. The old mine is still visited by the curious. With the price of gold what it is today, and by using modern equipment, it could very well pay to check this area further.

POTTER COUNTY - This legend, often mentioned by the Seneca Indians, is handed down from their elders. It concerns the lost treasure of Borie, valued at over $350,000 in gold. This is probably the least known large treasures in Pennsylvania.

Late in the 1690's, a small party of French Canadian voyageurs led by Louis Frontenac, left New Orleans by raft for the return trip to Montreal. They planned to travel up the Mississippi River to the Ohio River, then up the Allegheny, on to the Conewango and on to Chautauqua Lake in New York. From there they would go on the Prendergrast Creek to Lake Erie and on to Montreal.

The courer-de-bois left New Orleans on rafts loaded with provisions and a number of small kegs, each of which were loaded with gold coins covered with a thin film of gunpowder and anchored securely to the crude log transports by means of ropes and iron nails. The gold was to be delivered to His Most Gracious Majesty's Royal Governor in Montreal, and the party was instructed to guard the valuable cargo with their lives. Under no circumstances was it to fall into the hands of the English or the hated Senecas.

There was one difficulty other than the falls of the Upper Allegheny that the French couldn't discount, and that was the relentless warriors of the Seneca Nation, whose home the fair skinned Europeans were drawing near to.

It is believed that when the little band reached the area near what is now North Coudersport, the voyageurs and the priests decided that they would bury the kegs of gold, mark the site and continue as rapidly as possible toward the Genessee. They had been harassed throughout the upriver trip by Cornplanter and his warriors. So the legend goes, they turned south towards the valley now known as Borie. Near a huge rock which the Jesuits marked with a cross chiseled into the side, the scared Frenchmen buried the gold. A map was made of the location and they then headed back to the Allegheny and on to Canada. They reported to the exasperated governor that they had buried a tremendous treasure near a large rock somewhere near the head of the Allegheny. They had marked the site with a cross, explained the Jesuits.

For years the Senecas mentioned a rock in the Borie area that had a puzzling carving on its face. Since the carving had some religious significance, thought the Indians, they did not disturb it, or search for the hidden treasure, of which few were aware, until the return of the French to look for the buried loot which was not found.

It is a known fact that several historians mentioned the great rock, as did the Senecas. Few people have searched for it.

POTTER COUNTY - There were a number of Indians living in Potter County in the early days, and quite often they were seen to have pure silver ore in their possession. These Indians refused to give any information as to where they secured the metal and this caused the settlers to believe that the Indians knew of a deposit of silver somewhere in the mountains of Potter County. About the year 1894, a Cattaraugus Indian came to Coudersport. He was seen to walk off in the woods near the town of Sweden Valley and later return from the direction of what is now called Ice Mountain.

He was bearing a tied handkerchief, with some fine specimens of silver ore. After exhibiting this ore, he walked away without informing anyone as to his destination, where he came from, or how he obtained the ore. The result was quite obvious and natural, silver mining became the subject of conversation whenever two or more persons met, and a general search for the silver was made, but the mine's location was never learned.

POTTER COUNTY - During the 1800's, the main stage and mail road through this county was known as the Coudersport-Jersey Shore Turnpike. Several stagecoaches were robbed along this road. The Lewis and Connelly gangs, as well as other outlaws, operated in the area for a while. The Historical Society of Coudersport probably has information on this stretch of road.

SOMERSET COUNTY - On Laurel Ridge, near Jennerstown on the Westmoreland-Somerset County Line, lie several chests of gold and silver, hidden during the Civil War. These are buried or hidden in one of the numerous caves in the area. They have not been reported found. Many caches of guns and Civil War gear are stashed in the area also. Some of these have been recovered.

The gold and silver laden chests were supposedly buried by Colonel George Washington and General Braddock before the battle for Fort Duquesne in 1755. It is believed by many that Braddock's personal fortune was lost during the battle. Others think it was buried on Laurel Ridge before the battle.

UNION COUNTY - David Lewis, the outlaw, is supposed to have hidden a saddlebag containing $10,000 in gold behind a rock on the Juniata River south of Lewistown. When he returned to retrieve it, high water had washed it downstream. A very good write-up on the career of David Lewis was printed in the Daily News, November 8. 1947, by Albert M. Rung. Copies of this nine page article can be obtained from the office of the Daily News, Huntingdon, Pennsylvania, 16652.

VENANGO COUNTY - The oil Valley struck a pier of the Emblenton bridge on April 4, 1870, and sank a total loss. Two lives and all the cargo were lost.

VENANGO COUNTY - The Anne Lee was built in 1865 and sank in the ice near Oil City in the later 1860's, a total loss.

VENANGO COUNTY - About nine miles below Franklin, on the south side of the Allegheny River, is the site where one of the lead plates was buried by M. Celonon de Beinville, when he claimed all of the Northwest Territory for France in 1749. This plate has never been reported found.

VENANGO COUNTY - This location of lost diamonds would be worth investigating. Since it is recent, several people in the area still remember the incident.
  "Postal Inspector William Tafel has turned the Oil City Post Office into a diamond mine," wryly commented the Oil City, Pennsylvania, daily on November 22, 1928.
  The scourge of every mail fraud and cheat in the east, William Tafel, had been assigned to investigate the crash of an Air Mail Plane (a frequent occurrence in the late 1920's) and to collect its mail cargo. Sympathetic to the fate of the airmen, yet there was something sinister about Bill Tafel's attitude that puzzled many of the bystanders, who had rushed to the scene of the unfortunate accident, among them the horde of newswriters. Tafel 'clammed up' to every inquiry, and within an hour he had a cordon of guards around the scene of the accident, all armed to the teeth. Furthermore, he issued an ultimatum to the crowd to leave the scene. Not even a hunting owl or a fleeing rabbit could have penetrated Tafel's circle from any direction.
  To a handful of trusted confidants, standing in a clearing in rugged Bear Hollow, Tafel revealed in a very serious tone of voice that the mail plane en route from New York to Cleveland had six bags of registered mail, all of which contained diamonds consigned to midwestern jewel dealers. The shipment was worth a fortune, and would cost Uncle Sam an 'arm and a leg' should it not be found. Every bag was locked, however, the shrewd officer admitted that concussion could have l broken the locks, scattering diamonds the length of the hollow. The precious stones had to be accounted for, if it meant turning over every stone in Bear Hollow.
  Tafel had every off-duty postman in the Oil City region called to work, along with more agents sent from

Pittsburgh. Then the detective started what lead many to believe was America's greatest diamond hunt.

Tediously working over the earth, the postal clerks, many who would have a stiff back for days, found over 40 of the stones, a mere fraction of what the manifest showed. Final inventory showed 600 diamonds had been recovered, but the search was continued. Tafel would not say how many were never found.

Many believe it would have been a virtual impossibility for Tafel and his crew to have accounted for every diamond, no matter how thorough the search. That some were ground underfoot during the hours following the accident is almost a cinch. That a few may have been found in the half century that followed is a probability. If there are as many as ten of the stones left in Bear Hollow, it represents quite a small fortune, and diamonds are items that are not perishable.

For those interested in searching, the area is near Oil City, Pennsylvania.

WESTMORELAND COUNTY - The following excerpt is from "Braddock's Defeat" by Charles Hamilton, and was written by a servant of one of the officers killed in the battle:

"Satterday July ye 12th. We halted and broak and destroyed all the ammunition and provisions and buried them in the ground. The reason for destroying them was we wanted the wagons to carry the wounded. The horses dying so fast we was obliged to fire about a hundred(wagons) for want of hourse to draw them.

"Provisions that was so scarce about two days before became so plentiful that the men would hardly have anything but hams. I myself got six or eight it being as many as I could well carry on my horse. The men had the choice of all the wagons which could not be less than a hundred. All the provisions and wagons that could not be taken with us was set on fire to hinder them falling into enemy hands."

There have been conflicting versions of this story but it is believed that this cache of supplies is buried about 38 miles southeast of Pittsburgh, in Westmoreland County. Local research could pay off on this one.

THE BOON ROAD

I enclose this short story of an early road, built by white men in Pennsylvania (because it is so little known) and for the benefit of historians and treasure hunters that would like to further pursue the subject of early French occupation in Pennsylvania.

The Boon Road has never had more than local publicity and few recognized historians have ever heard of it, but it definitely was a part of the French and Indian War and of early French occupation in Pennsylvania.

When the first settlers arrived in what is now Warren McKean, Potter and Clinton Counties, Pennsylvania, during the early 1800's, they found a well-built road. There were dugways on the hillsides and places where fords had been made. Deep wheel ruts were visible, holes had been filled in with rock, in all, it was a very good road that ran for 130 miles through virgin timber and mountains. The pioneers had no idea who had made it.

Lengthy research has shown that the road was built in 1756, by a French army on their way to attack the English Fort Augusta at the junction of the North Branch

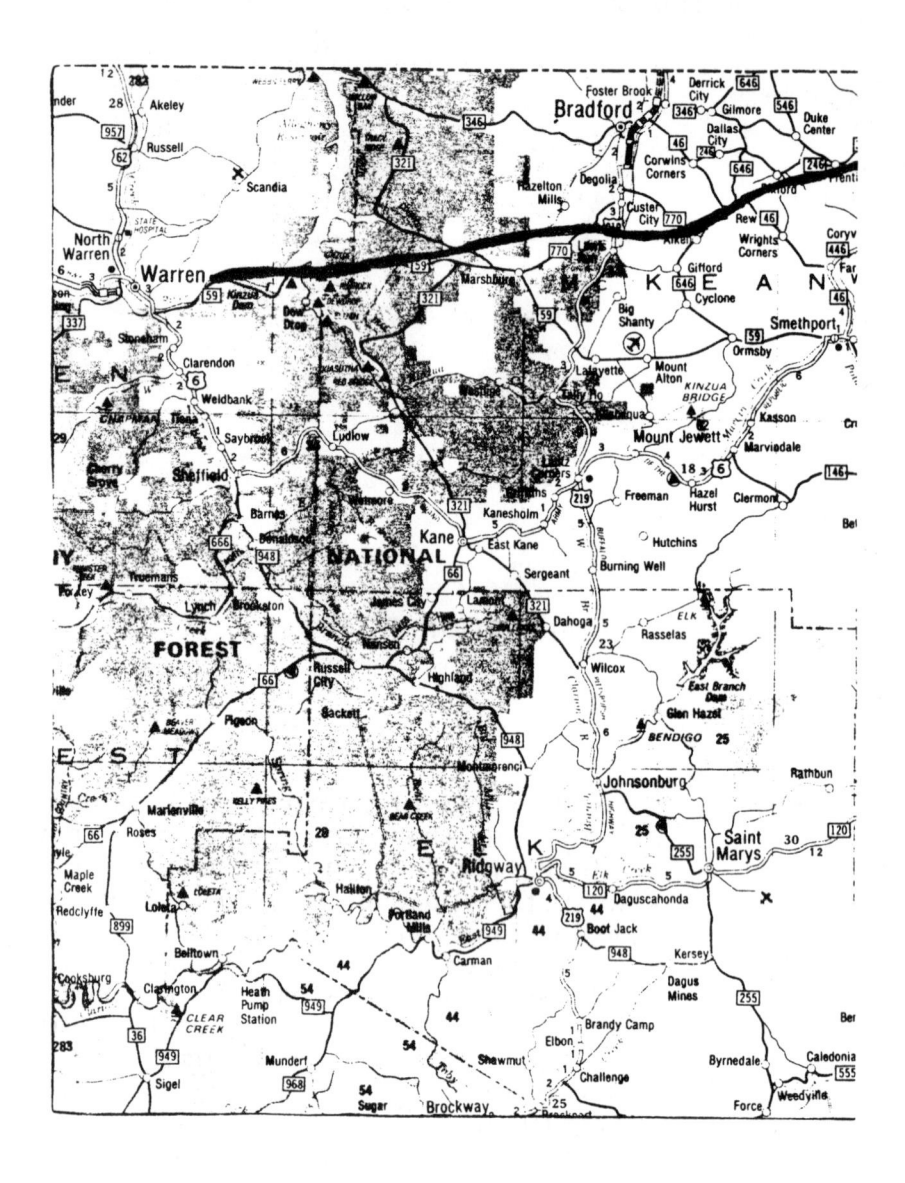

This route roughly follows the path of the Boon
Road through Warren, McKean, Potter and Clinton
Counties, Pennsylvania.

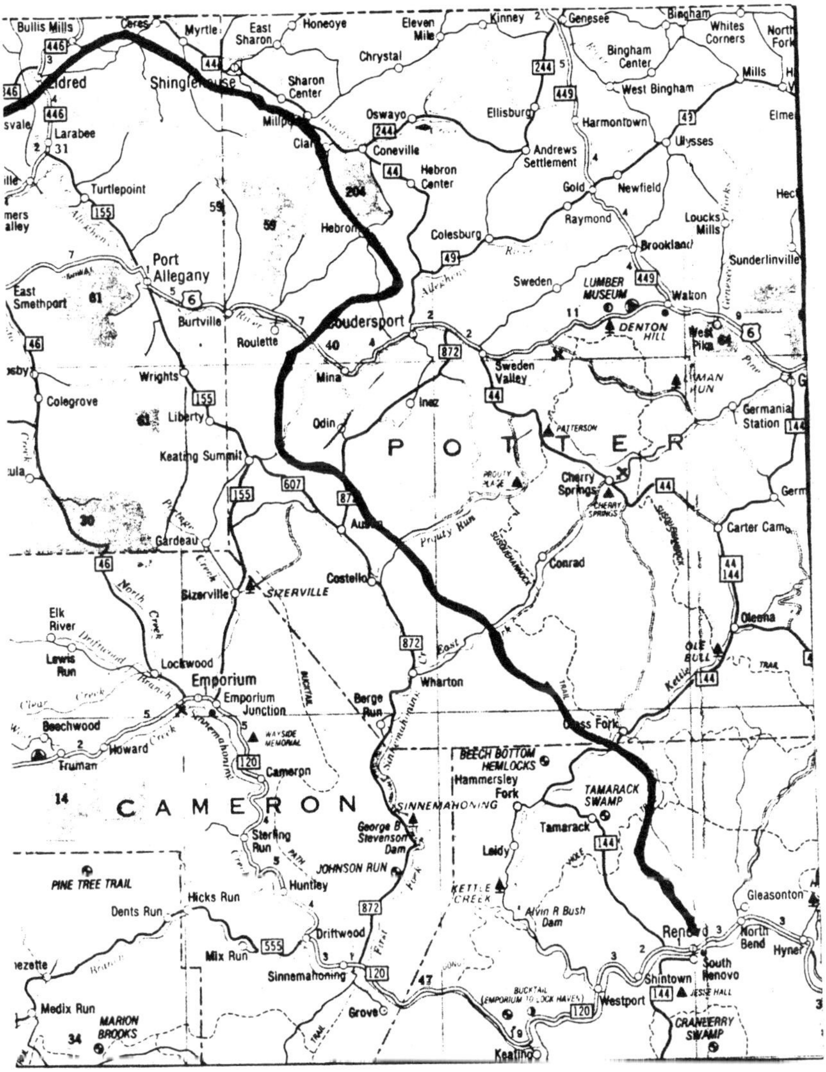
Bullis Mills
Ceres
Myrtle
East Sharon
Honeoye
Eleven Mile
Kinney
Genesee
Bingham
Whites Corners
North Fork
Chrystal
Bingham Center
Mills
Shinglehouse
Sharon Center
West Bingham
Larabee
Oswayo
Ellisburg
Harmontown
Ulysses
Coneville
Andrews Settlement
Hebron Center
Turtlepoint
Gold
Newfield
Raymond
Loucks Mills
Hebron
Colesburg
Brookland
Port Allegany
Sunderlinville
East Smethport
Sweden
LUMBER MUSEUM
Walton
Burtville
Roulette
Coudersport
DENTON HILL
West Pike
Mina
Sweden Valley
Wrights
Colegrove
Inez
Germania Station
Liberty
Odin
PATTERSON
P O T T E R
Keating Summit
Cherry Springs
CHERRY SPRINGS
PROUTY PLACE
Austin
Carter Camp
Prouty Run
Gardeau
Conrad
Costello
Sizerville
SIZERVILLE
Elk River
Ole Bull
Lewis Run
Lockwood
Emporium
Emporium Junction
Wharton
Berge Run
Cross Fork
Beechwood
Howard
Truman
WAYSIDE MEMORIAL
Cameron
BEECH BOTTOM HEMLOCKS
Hammersley Fork
TAMARACK SWAMP
Tamarack
C A M E R O N
SINNEMAHONING
Sterling Run
George B Stevenson Dam
Leidy
JOHNSON RUN
PINE TREE TRAIL
Huntley
Hicks Run
KETTLE CREEK
Gleasonton
Dents Run
Alvin R Bush Dam
Renovo
North Bend
Hyner
Driftwood
Mix Run
South Renovo
Shintown
Sinnemahoning
JESSE HALL
BUCKTAIL (EMPORIUM TO LOCK HAVEN)
Westport
Medix Run
Grove
CRANBERRY SWAMP
MARION BROOKS
Keating

and West Branch of the Susquehanna River. The French army never got there and the battle was never fought.

The Boon Road had its origin in the Indian town of Kanaoriangon (Warren, Pa.). It came through Warren and McKean Counties to Ceres, then up the Oswayo Valley to Millport, then over Nigger Hill and across Crandall Hill, passing one half mile north of the Five Corners Cemetery, then down Steer Brook to the Allegheny valley. There it turned west and crossed the river about half a mile west of Frinks, then up to Prosser Hallow to the highland on Sweden Hill, passing near Chase's Corners and on across Denton Hill, then down one of the branches of Pine Creek, up Hopper House Hollow and across the Jersey Shore Turnpike. Then down what is still on maps as Boon Run (Where part of the old road bed can be found) to Cross Fork Creek. Then probably up Cherry Run and down Ole Bull Run to Kettle Creek, then down that valley into Clinton County, leaving Kettle Creek at Haystack Hollow (also known as Hogstock Hollow). It apparently went along the east side of Tamarack Swamp and then down Drury Run. The old road bed can still be found on the opposite side of the creek from the public road. Then it turned eastward upon the highland and followed what is shown as the Boon Road on the Tamarack Quadrangle of a topographic map, then on to Renovo.

The French Army came to the West Branch of the Susquehanna River where it is the furthest north, and the nearest for them. It is reasonable to believe that this was the army who built the Boon Road, made boats at Renovo and started down the river. For the story of what happened next we have items from old history books, none of which mention the road.

"The French Invasion of Western Pennsylvania, 1753" by Donald H. Kent is a very good source of information on the early occupation of Pennsylvania by the French.

In "Report of the Commission to Locate the Site of the Frontier Forts of Pennsylvania," volume one, page 355, it says that after peace came, the friendly Indians told the English at Fort Augusta that in the fall of 1756, a party of French and Indians left the lake country to attack Fort Augusta. After they came to the headwaters of the West Branch of the Susquehanna, they descended by water to about the mouth of Loyalsock Creek. There they landed and sent scouts ahead to look over Fort Augusta, then partially built. They reported the fort was very strong and well guarded and considered it imprudent to attack. The French had only 4 small brass canon, too light to break down the heavy walls of the fort. These they dumped into a deep pot hole at the upper end of the old raceground island, which has been known as the Cannon Hole ever since. The army returned without showing up at Fort Augusta.

This same tale appears in Otzinachson History of the West Branch, revised edition of 1889, by J.R. Meginness on page 214. Few have believed the story because they knew nothing about the Boon Road and could not understand how the French moved cannon to the river from forts near Lake Erie. Tradition has a way of upsetting recorded history and turning out to be more accurate than it first appears. This story has the ring of truth, makes sense and explains why the Boon Road was built.

Directly after the tale of the Cannon Hole in Maginness' history, there is a letter from Marquis deVaudreuil to M. deMoras in Canada, dated July 13, 1757. In this report of the military news in the Pennsylvania area he mentions the scouting party who decided that Fort Augusta was too strong for a French Army to take. He said nothing about building a road, an army going down the river or the loss of 4 valuable cannon. It is plain to see that he did not want his superior officers in Canada to know about such a great waste of time and money.

Furthermore, Vaudreuil and his associate, Joncaire, must have known all about the strength of Fort Augusta long before they sent the army down the river. Their many French and Indian scouts watched every move the English were making. They were seen almost daily on the hills overlooking Fort Augusta. It appears that the actual purpose of sending an army was to build a road for personal gain in the fur trade with the Indians.

William A. Hunter, in his "Forts on the Pennsylvania Frontier" page 518 says: "90 or 100 friendly Indians arrived by way of the North Branch on 13 March 1757, and stayed at Fort Augusta for 4 days. A few hours after their departure a second party of 30 or 40 more Indians arrived. In formal council of 18 March, the chiefs of this second party confirmed the story already reported by the preceding group, that 800 French and Indians were preparing to descend the West Branch."

"On 7 April, Major Burd sent Captain Patterson and 10 men up the West Branch in search of the reported enemy force. This party, which returned on 25 April, found Clearfield deserted and largly burnt and found no trace or track of the enemy."

On page 522: "In June Lieut. Col. Weiser heard that the enemy had cut a road to within 10 miles of Fort Augusta. Captain Hambright had a company of men set out on 26 June to explore the country for 20 miles around. They found nothing."

No wonder the scouts from Fort Augusta found no French Army. They were several months too late. No wonder that the records of Fort Augusta made no mention of the Boon Road or an invasion toward them by a French Army. They never knew the danger they were in.

This retreat over the Boon Road was the beginning of the end of the French claims in Pennsylvania. On 27 of November 1758, the French evacuated Fort Duquesne when they learned the British General, John Forbes, was very close with a force of over 6,000 men. The next day Forbes took possession. The next year in August, they abandoned Fort LeBoeuf, leaving all of Pennsylvania under English control.

The mystery of who built the Boon Road is solved. It required research to learn that it was an army of Frenchmen who built it. No one else but the Indians were here at that time. At first the knowledge was a closely guarded secret and it became a tantalizing mystery because of the lack of French records concerning the road. Those interested in more research will find the answers in the greed of certain French officers. This also explains why there are no French records.

The French officer who appears to have been the most concerned with the building of the Boon Road was Chadbert Joncaire. His friend and close associate was Marquis deVaudreuil. These men like many others in the French army were more interested in building up personal fortunes for themselves than they were in protecting the interests of their king. They did not hesitate to use his supplies and his army for their own purpose. Vaudreuil told Joncaire that if he had unexpected losses in his fur trade he could charge them to the account of the crown.

Joncaire was the most influential man in this entire region. He assumed the task of provisioning about 40 posts and villages. He was a large employer of labor and built storehouses at several towns among the Seneca Indians and in the Allegheny valley. He filled them with vast quantities of goods and carried on a fur business with the Indians.

It is recorded that the Niagara portage road was built under Joncaire's direction. Proof is lacking but he may be the man who directed the building of the Boon Road over the mountains to the valley of the West Branch. What he wanted was a good road so he could extend his fur trading business into the West Branch of the Susquehanna area.

Joncaire lived for a time with his family in Montreal. Late in 1761, he crossed over to France where he was promptly arrested and confined in the Bastille together with the 20 other army officers, including Vaudreuil.

After two years of proceedings in a Paris Court, the verdict was announced. Many were stripped of their wealth by huge fines. Vaudreuil was acquitted for lack of evidence. Joncaire was found guilty "of having examined inconsiderately and without scrutiny the inventories of provisions in the fort where he commanded," and was forbidden to do it again.

Joncaire returned to his home in Montreal. He took an oath of allegiance to Great Britian and was permitted to continue his fur trade with the Indians, under the watchful eyes of the authorities. He had a post at Detroit where he died.

No one knows how the road came to be called Boon, unless it is a corruption of the French word bon, which means good, for it was a well built road. By using a modern map this road would not be hard to find and trace. It could be a relic hunters dream for someone with a metal detector.

TREASURE CHEST FOUND

This treasure find should be of interest to anyone that wants to investigate the Boon Road. Chadbert Joncaire is known to have buried other chests that have not been reported found. (Some of which could be along the Boon Road.) About 40 miles south of Fort LeBouef the French had Fort Machault at what is now Franklin, Venango County, Pennsylvania. This site was selected by Captain Chadbert de Joncaire, who commanded the fort for a time.

For many years there was a tradition in Franklin that there was a buried treasure left by the French when they abandoned Fort Machault.

Columbus Brown lived in Franklin at the time. He had a mania in regard to the treasure and searched for it for years without success. Finally, he got the answer in a dream, or a vision. He was informed by a man with a foreign accent, dressed in a military uniform, that if he would measure a certain distance from the center of a rock in the creek, due north, and then measure 33 feet due west from that point, he would find the treasure at the foot of a large tree. The next morning he went with pick and shovel to the owner of the field and got permission to dig there.

In two hours time he came to an iron chest. It was nearly two-thirds full of gold and silver coins. They were mostly French, but a number of English, German and Spanish coins were among the lot. They were dated from 1729 to 1754, which was the year Fort Machault was completed. On a brass ruler found in the chest the name of Joncaire was plainly stamped. He was in command of the troops. The fort was hastily evacuated in July 1759.

The field where the chest was found was about 75 rods west of the fort. Mr. Brown had found a treasure chest of about $27,000, a good sized fortune in Joncaire's day. Many of the coins were later on display at the local banks.

Look closely for the remains of the old roads in these two pictures.

The author shows you a couple of examples of metal detecting sites.

METAL DETECTOR SITES

METAL DETECTOR SITES IN PENNSYLVANIA

This section on metal detector sites is for relic or artifact hunting only. A person might find a few coins, or a cache, but the primary reason for searching is to find historic relics.

The listing under each county gives the names of communities, villages and settlements in Pennsylvania by Indians, French, British and Americans from its earliest history, the locations of which are believed to be within that particular county. The records in each county seat are usually the best sources of information on a ghost or near ghost town. Local historical societies, libraries and senior citizens can also be of invaluable aid in helping to locate these former communities.

It is emphasized that these possible ghost towns, et cetera, in some instances may not be ghosts at all, but survive today under names different than their originals. Many community names were changed as a matter of pride, the once common "ville", "burg" or "borough" being dropped as communities grew larger in size. Others had their names changed because their originals were just not satisfactory to later generations of inhabitants, and some were forced to change their names by post office officials to eliminate confusing duplication. The end of a war eliminated the necessity for many military installations.

Many of these pioneer communities were nothing more than a few houses and a store or two cluttered around a mill, lumber camp, a ferry landing, stream ford or fort or along an early railroad. As these physical features disappeared with the settlement of the country, so did many of the communities. On the other hand, some of these early settlements were simply absorbed by faster growing neighboring towns, thus losing their identities, their sites engulfed today by urban areas.

While not all the possible ghosts listed herein will turn out to be true ghosts, many among them will be genuine ghosts--completely vanished and forgotten. Possibly the sites of some of the latter have never been searched for artifacts, and are thus virgin fields for metal detectors.

Pennsylvania, being one of the oldest settled states of the Union with its almost countless number of locations of French, English and early American settlements, forts, trading posts, battlegrounds and miles of rivers, make it especially attractive to lovers of the past.

Its important historic sites and large population for almost three hundred years make it a relic hunter's dream. The County Court Clerks, Historical Societies, state offices and libraries have been especially helpful during the completion of this treasure guide for the Keystone State.

ADAMS COUNTY - South of Heidlesburg is where the Studebakers first had a wagon shop in 1830. Later they moved west and became the forerunners in the automotive industry.

ADAMS COUNTY - The Lutheran Church in Fairfield served as a hospital after the battle between Confederate and Union troops at Gettysburg on July 1-2, 1863.

ADAMS COUNTY - The Battle of Gettysburg, July of 1863, was the turning point of the Civil War. Although the immediate area of the battlefield is now a National Park, there are quite a few farms nearby that had action on them. These are privately owned and might allow treasure hunters to look for relics. The Union lost over 9,000 men and the Confederate forces lost over 17,000 men, not counting the wounded.

ADAMS COUNTY - At Hunterstown on July 2, 1863, Union and Confederate soldiers met in a small skirmish.

ADAMS COUNTY - On July 3 and 4, 1863, Confederate and Union troops clashed at Fairfield, a short distance from Gettysburg.

ADAMS COUNTY - Near the Gettysburg battlefield is an area known as the Indian field. Tradition has it that a large Indian village with a French trading post was located here in the 1750's. A large Indian battle was fought here and the Indian dead were buried in the area.

ALLEGHENY COUNTY - Shannopin Town, an Indian village, was located near where Lawrenceville is today. The village lasted from about 1731 until 1754.

ALLEGHENY COUNTY - At Monroeville is the site of the last base of General Forbes army before they entered Fort Duquesne on November 25, 1758.

ALLEGHENY COUNTY - An early Indian village, called Chartier's Town, was located near where Tarentum is today.

ALLEGHENY COUNTY - Bouquest Camp, located east of Pittsburgh, was the supply base for Forbes Campaign of 1758, to take Fort Duquesne.

ALLECHENY COUNTY - Southeast of Wilkensburg is the site where General Braddock and his British forces were defeated on July 9, 1755, by the French and Indians of Fort Duquesne.

ALLEGHENY COUNTY - About fifteen miles below Pittsburgh is where Logstown, an Indian village and later a trading post, was located. Christopher Gist and George Washington had camped here for a week about 1758.

ARMSTRONG COUNTY - Fort Armstrong was built in June 1779, about two miles south of where Kittanning is today. By late fall of the same year it had been abandoned because of the Indians.

ARMSTRONG COUNTY - Blanket Hill, east of Kittanning received its name because of the blankets left here by the Armstrong expedition after they destroyed Kittanning, an Indian village in 1756. Troops also stopped here on September 7, 1756, while fighting Indians.

ARMSTRONG COUNTY - One of the first and largest iron works in the area was Brady's Bend Works. They were in operation from 1839 until 1873.

ARMSTRONG COUNTY - Kaylor once had a population of over 5,000 during the oil and coal boom. Today only a few houses are left.

ARMSTRONG COUNTY – Ask the County Clerk at Kittanning for information on Slate Lick and Elderton, neither one has a postoffice today.

BEAVER COUNTY – About a mile below the mouth of Big Beaver Creek is where an old Delaware Indian village stood. In 1756, the French had a trading post here, with several buildings. This was all abandoned at the close of the French and Indian War in 1763.

BEAVER COUNTY – On the northeast side of Ambridge is the site of Logstown a large Indian village in 1727 and lasting until 1758.

BEAVER COUNTY – Fort McIntosh was the first U.S Military post north of the Ohio. It was located where Beaver is today, in 1778. In 1791, the fort was abandoned.

BEAVER COUNTY – General Anthony Wayne's army camped north of where Ambridge is today, from Nov. 1792 until April 1793, before they moved west for the Battle of Fallen Timbers.

BEDFORD COUNTY – Entrenchments are still visible south of Loysburg that were built in June 1863, for protection against Confederate forces which were threatening the area.

BEDFORD COUNTY – Fort Bedford was built about 1758, a trading post was also established here. The fort was the base for the Forbes and Boquest expeditions.

BEDFORD COUNTY – West of Schellsburg was located Shawnee Cabins Camp, used by General Forbes in 1758 in his fight against the French at Fort Duquesne. An Indian village had been here earlier.

BEDFORD COUNTY – A small stockade called Fort Juniata was erected in 1758, just east of where Everett is today.

BEDFORD COUNTY - Fort Littleton, used during the French and Indian War, had over one hundred officers and men stationed there in 1758.

BEDFORD COUNTY - Werefordsburg, no longer on the maps, had about fifteen houses, store and tavern at one time.

BEDFORD COUNTY - The near-ghost town of Juniata Crossing had a tavern built in 1818 that was a popular stage stop for several years and a postoffice. Both are gone now.

BEDFORD COUNTY - Check at Bedford for the location of Schellsburg and St. Clairsville, two near-ghost towns.

BERKS COUNTY - In the lower part of the county were seven iron forges, no longer in use. Ruins of many of them can still be seen.

BERKS COUNTY - After Burgoyne's surrender in 1777, some of the German mercenaries, called Hessians, were brought here as prisoners and held from 1781 until 1783. The camp was a group of huts on a hill, one fourth mile north of Reading, on U.S. 422.

BERKS COUNTY - A log building, erected in 1750, was a trading post operated by Conrad Weiser. This post was located near where Reading is today.

BERKS COUNTY - The ruins of an iron furnace built prior to 1800 are located near Robesonia.

BERKS COUNTY - About two miles south of Reading at the tip of Fritts Island, are the remains of the eastern most lock of Union Canal, built in 1828 and used until 1884.

BERKS COUNTY - Fort Henry was built in 1756, about two miles from where Bethel is today, and was a garrisoned fort with troops during the French and Indian War.

BERKS COUNTY - About one mile east of Bernville are two locks, remains of the Union Canal, used from 1828 until 1884.

BERKS COUNTY - Remains of a tow path of the Union Canal can be found southeast of Mt. Pleasant along the Tulpehoken Creek.

BERKS COUNTY - Goughersville, once a bustling village has only an old cemetery and about a dozen old frame houses left. All the stores and the postoffice are gone.

BERKS COUNTY - Maiden Creek, a near-ghost town, once had an inn that was a stagecoach stop for many years. A deserted Friends meeting house that was built in 1759 and moved to the present site in 1934, has not been used for several years. The postoffice has been closed.

BERKS COUNTY - Maxatowny, once a thriving industrial town with mines, foundry, boot, shoe and carpet factories, has become nothing more than a small farming settlement. All these factories and mines are gone.

BERKS COUNTY - Data may be obtained in Reading on Lenhartsville, Bethel and Hereford, all near-ghost towns.

BLAIR COUNTY - In Altoona are the remains of an iron furnace built in 1811 and operated until 1884.

BLAIR COUNTY - Fort Roberdeau was a Revolutionary War fort, located about one mile south of where Culp is today. The fort was built in 1778 to protect the Sinking Valley lead mines.

BLAIR COUNTY - Assunepachla, a Delaware-Shawnee Indian village, was located east of Hollidaysburg before 1748. A trading post was here as early as 1734.

BLAIR COUNTY - Near Hollidaysburg are the ruins of several charcoal iron furnaces and forges built and used in the period between 1790 and 1850.

BLAIR COUNTY - Etna Furnace was built in 1809, about one half mile east of where Yellow Springs is today. The furnace was used until 1877. The stack and some of the stone buildings still remain.

BLAIR COUNTY - Ore Hill started when iron was discovered nearby, later a saw mill was built and operated until 1927. Nothing is left of this village today.

BLAIR COUNTY - Inquire at Altoona for the location of Reese and Canoe Creek, both deserted lumber camps.

BRADFORD COUNTY - About two miles south of Athens is where Queen Esther's Town, a Munsee Indian village was located. In 1778 the town was burned by soldiers.

BRADFORD COUNTY - Friendshuetten, a Moravian mission, was located at Wyalusing. A modern Indian town, it was founded in 1763. The town and mission were abandoned in 1772, because of Indian trouble.

BRADFORD COUNTY - Athens is located where the Indian town of Tioga was located. Tioga was destroyed in 1778 and many relics have been found in the area.

BRADFORD COUNTY - Near Athens was the site of Fort Sullivan, built in August of 1770. It was a base for the Central New York Campaign.

BRADFORD COUNTY - About four and one-half miles east of Wyalusing is Indian Hill, where on September 29, 1778, a battle between men from Muncy and the Indians took place.

BRADFORD COUNTY - Just inside the state line, about .3 miles off U.S. 220, is the remains of a three-quarters mile of earthworks and the ruins of an Indian village that was shown on Champlains map of 1632. This is located on what is known as Spanish Hill.

BRADFORD COUNTY - Near Canton is the shell of Crocket Lodge, so named because it was the home of Frank Mayo (1839-86), an actor who played David

Crockett on the stage. The building has been unoccupied for several years and is falling into ruin. A mineral spring nearby drew many of Mayo's fellow actors into the area in the late 1800's.

BRADFORD COUNTY - Near Runnerfield is the site of Asylum (French Azilum), a deserted town established for aristocratic French refugees of the French Revolution in 1792. La Grande Mansion was built, supposedly for Louis XVI and Marie Antoinette, but they were never able to use it. There were about fifty houses, shops, a chapel, schoolhouse and a market. When Napoleon granted amnesty in 1802, most of the people returned to France and the town returned to wilderness.

BRADFORD COUNTY - Laquin was once a coal and lumber center. At one time there were over 1,000 people living there, a hotel, saw mill, chemical factory, stave mill, veneer plant and stores. By 1941 it had become a ghost town.

BRADFORD COUNTY - Information can be obtained at Towanda on Dushore, Standing Stone, Sheshequin, Fassett and Columbia Crossroads, all near-ghost towns.

BUCKS COUNTY - Lock #12 of the Delaware Canal was located at Lumbersville with an aquaduct nearby.

BUCKS COUNTY - At New Hope were several locks of the Delaware Canal and the only toll station between Bristol and Easton. The Jerrico Creek aquaduct is located nearby. The station was called River House and was built in 1794. South of New Hope the highway crosses where the canal was.

BUCKS COUNTY - Durham Furnace had a revival of the iron industry when the Delaware Canal went through the area. The furnace operated from 1848 until 1908. Lock #21 was located here.

BUCKS COUNTY - The Delaware Canal which ran the length of Bucks County would be a good area to check. It was opened to travel in 1832 and was used to haul coal to Philadelphia and goods to the coal regions on the return trip. Just prior to the Civil War, a million tons of coal were carried each year. At one time 3,000 barges were in operation on the canal. The last barge made the journey in 1931.

BUCKS COUNTY - The Old Ferry Inn still stands on the northern side of Route 532, near Washington Crossing Bridge, over the Delaware River. Washington and his staff camped near this site in 1776. It is believed the earliest part of the inn was constructed about 1774 and the present additions made in 1780 or 1790.

BUCKS COUNTY - Check at Doylesville for the locations of these almost deserted villages: Aqualong, a crossroads hamlet without a postoffice: Holocong, Kentersville postoffice discontinued; Uhlertown: and Montgomery Square, no longer a postoffice.

BUTLER COUNTY - The old Stone House was built by John Brown in 1822. It is located on Route #8, north of Butler, and was a well known stagecoach stop. General Lafayette and other notables stopped here.

BUTLER COUNTY - The County Clerk at Butler can help with the location of Portersville, Glade Mill and Middle Lancaster. The last two no longer have postoffices.

CAMBRIA COUNTY - Near South Fork was the village of Mineral Point, washed away by the Johnstown Flood in 1889. The town was not rebuilt.

CAMBRIA COUNTY - Dunlo, a near ghost town, had a saw mill started in 1792. The mill operated until 1908.

CAMBRIA COUNTY - Allendale was a saw mill camp from 1896 until 1908, today nothing is left.

CAMBRIA COUNTY - St. Michael, now a ghost town, developed where Lake Conemaugh was, on the site of the abandoned South Fork Fishing and Hunting Club. It is located about one mile south of the town of South Fork. The dam that was here broke in 1889 and was the cause of the Johnstown Flood. The Club abandoned their buildings shortly after the flood because of hard feelings of the citizens in the communities destroyed by the flood.

CAMBRIA COUNTY - Data can be obtained from the County Clerk at Edenburg on the location of Beulah, a town founded by Rev. Morgan John Rhys, in 1796. All that remains of the town today is the cemetery.

CAMERON COUNTY - The Allegheny Portage, which went from the West Branch of the Susquehanna River to the Allegheny River ran from east of Emporium twenty-three miles to Portage Creek, where Port Allegheny is today. Here travel by water was resumed.

CAMERON COUNTY - Two deserted lumber camps are Busters camp on Indian Camp Run, and one unnamed on Elk Fork Run.

CAMERON COUNTY - Cameron, once a thriving lumber town, now has only about ten houses left. The postoffice has been discontinued. It is located on U.S. 120 out of Emporium.

CAMERON COUNTY - Hicks Run, a ghost town, has nothing left but a cemetery, one house and several hunting camps. At one time one of the biggest sawmills in Pennsylvania was here. There was a postoffice, hotel, pool room, barber shop, school, three boarding houses, store and about ninety houses. There were several lumber camps located nearby. In 1912 the mills closed and several of the buildings were moved to nearby towns. By 1930 most of the houses that were left were vacant.

CAMERON COUNTY - Inquire at Emporium for the location of Driftwood.

CARBON COUNTY - Near Lehighton is the site of Gnadenhuetten, a Moravian Mission, built in 1746, for the Mahikan-Delaware Indians. On November 24, 1755, Munsee Indians burned the mission, killing many of the Delaware Indians. The mission was never rebuilt.

CAMERON COUNTY - Sterling Run (A near-ghost town) has only a few permanent residents and a few hunting cabins. At one time over a thousand people lived here. There was a huge sawmill that employed, with the timber cutting, several hundred lumber jacks. In May of 1894, a huge forest fire almost completely wiped out the town. When the fire destroyed the surrounding timber, the town died.

The great mill pond is now overgrown with wild milkweeds and mullein. Only a trained eye can pick out the outlines of the streets of the community that once boasted hotels, restaurants, boarding houses, the lumber mill and dozens of stores.

When the lumber-jacks came into Sterling Run on pay day, money flowed like water. The site of the ghost town should be a natural for coinshooters. It would be difficult to comprehend the number of glass insulators, bottles and other artifacts of the last century that remain buried in the woods and fields that once was a hustling bustling frontier lumber town.

CARBON COUNTY -- Fort Allen was built in 1756, where Weissport is today. It was one of a series of forts built during the French and Indian War. All that remains of the fort is the well.

CARBON COUNTY - Information may be obtained at Jim Thorpe on the location of Lehigh Gap, the postoffice has been discontinued.

CENTER COUNTY - There were three early forts in this county, Lowell, Watsons, and Upper Fort. The Aaronburg Historical Museum has information on their location and history.

CENTRE COUNTY - Southeast of Centre Hall was Potter's Fort, built in 1777, with a solid stockade giving refuge to settlers for miles around.

CENTRE COUNTY - At Milesburg was a Delaware Indian village named Woapalanne or "Bald Eagle". Indians from here raided the frontier during the Revolutionary War.

CENTRE COUNTY - Near Curtlin was the Eagle Iron Works, built about 1810 and operated until 1922. A few remains can still be seen.

CENTRE COUNTY - Near Port Matilda are ruins of several charcoal iron furnaces and forges built and used between 1790 and 1850. Very little remains.

CENTRE COUNTY - A sandy area north of Boalsburg, known as the Barrens was worked for iron ore in colonial times. In 1881 the Carnegie Brothers established an iron center known as Scotia here, they erected houses, set up machinery and built a railroad. The town is now gone, the roads are overgrown and almost impassable.

CENTRE COUNTY - Ask at Bellefonte for directions to Potters Mills, Acemann and Martha's Furnace, all have lost their postoffices, and Woodware, all are now near-ghost towns.

CHESTER COUNTY - At Chester Springs, once a popular resort, was where Washington had his headquarters after the Battle of Brandywine. During the winter of 1777-1778, when the forces camped at Valley Forge, a hospital was set up here.

CHESTER COUNTY - Valley Forge was where General Washington and his troops had their winter camp in 1777-1778. The British Army had burned the village in the fall of 1777.

CHESTER COUNTY - The Warwick Iron Mine, near St. Mary's is nothing but ruins today, it was built in 1737. At one time this area had several working mines, with the Hopewell mine nearby, and the French Creek mine a mile or two away. None of these mines have been worked ince 1920's.

CHESTER COUNTY - The near ghost town of Slymar is located on the Pennsylvania-Maryland border. The postoffice has been discontinued.

CHESTER COUNTY - The County Clerk can give information on a settlement that used to exist in southern Chester County. It had a cotton mill, postoffice and several houses. It's most common name was Borough of Hopewell.

CHESTER COUNTY - Ask for directions to Brandywine and Compass, in Chester, nothing but small hamlets with their postoffice--now closed.

CLARION COUNTY - East of Allensburg is the Buchanan Furnace, built in 1844 and abandoned in 1858.

CLARION COUNTY - Northeast of Clarion can still be seen parts of Helen Furnace, built in 1845 and used until 1867.

CLARION COUNTY - Data can be obtained at Clarion on the location of Cranberry, Leeper and Lucinda, all slowly dying towns.

CLEARFIELD COUNTY - Thousands of arrow heads and axes, hoes and other Indian artifacts have been recovered at Lecountes Mills on the West Branch of the Susquehanna River. Many more artifacts are waiting to be found along the river in what is known as "bottom land".

CLEARFIELD COUNTY - Chicklacamoose, an Indian village, was located near Clearfield. It was still in existence in 1758.

CLEARFIELD COUNTY - Southwest of Luthersburg is a former camping place of the Indians, where the junction of two or their paths crossed. These were the Great Shamokin and the Venango Paths. During the War of 1812 American troops camped here for several days.

CLEARFIELD COUNTY - Near Karthaus was an iron furnace built in 1817 and abandoned in 1839.

CLINTON COUNTY - In Lock Haven is the site of Fort Reed, a stockaded house that was built in the 1770's, and used for several years.

CLINTON COUNTY - Drury's Run, once the site of two large brick plants and a large population with a promise of a great future is deserted. Today the kilns resemble large beehives.

CLINTON COUNTY - Keating, a thriving lumber town at once time, has but four or five houses today. Cattle graze where once spike-booted lumberjacks walked the dusty streets.

CLINTON COUNTY -Westport and Cooks's Run, both mere shadows of their former greatness, lie west of Keating. Both communities are rarely visited anymore except by deer hunters and trout fishermen. Only a few decades back, Westport was one of the most prosperous communities along the Susquehanna.

CLINTON COUNTY - In the Susquehanna River, northeast of Lock Haven is an island where many Indian nations camped or lived at different times. Many different types of Indian artifacts can be found here.

CLINTON COUNTY - Fort Horn, a stockaded log house was located about four miles northeast of Lock Haven in 1777. In 1778 the fort was abandoned because of Indian trouble.

CLINTON COUNTY - Lock Haven was the end of the West Branch Division of the Pennsylvania Canal, built in 1834. Bald Eagle Cross-Cut Canal joined here with two locks, a dam and a towpath.

CLINTON COUNTY - Cammal was established in 1889 and was a merging point for our railroads during lumbering heydays. There was a mill, several churches, department store, bakery and meat store. By 1904 the mill was gone and today the town is almost deserted.

CLINTON COUNTY - Queens Run, a ghost town, once had a large fire brick company. Today it does not even appear on the map.

CLINTON COUNTY - Farrandsville has only a few people left of the once busy village. A fire brick company located a plant here and a small railroad was built. Both of these are gone today.

CLINTON COUNTY - The town of Glen Union was once a busy spot with a saw mill, church, school and an extensive logging railroad network. Now only a few houses are left.

CLINTON COUNTY - Gleasonton, a near-ghost town today, at one time had a saw mill, boarding house, two hotels and several homes. When the mills closed about 1905, the town began to die.

COLUMBIA COUNTY - Cataweissa, an Indian village, was located near where the town of Catawissa is today.

COLUMBIA COUNTY - About one mile northeast of Bloomsburg is where Fort Wheeler was built in 1778. The fort lasted until the Revolutionary War was over.

COLUMBIA COUNTY - About six miles northeast of Bloomsburg was the site of Fort Jenkins, a stockaded house built in 1778. It was used until 1780, when the Indians attacked and it was destroyed.

COLUMBIA COUNTY - In Bloomsburg is the site of Fort McClure, a stockade erected after Fort Jenkins was destroyed in 1780.

CRAWFORD COUNTY - South of Adamsville, the bed of the Erie Extension Canal can still be seen close to the railroad.

CRAWFORD COUNTY - North of Conneautville is part of the old channel, near the highway, of the Erie Extension Canal, finished in 1843-44 and used til 1871.

CRAWFORD COUNTY - West of Sherman can be seen the remains of the bed of the Erie Extension Canal. The canal ran beside where the railroad track is today.

CRAWFORD COUNTY - Information can be obtained in Meadville on the location of Hartstown, near-ghost town.

CUMBERLAND COUNTY - Laughlin Mill was built about 1763 and was used until sometime in the late 1890's.

CUMBERLAND COUNTY - In Shippensburg is the site of Fort Morris, built in July of 1755. Later the fort was garrisoned by provincial troops.

CUMBERLAND COUNTY - At Lemoyne can still be seen remains of brestworks built before the battle of Gettysburg. On June 29, 1863, a few Confederate scouts came near Fort Couch, as the breastworks were called, but withdrew without firing a shot.

CUMBERLAND COUNTY - In the early 1700's, about 1718 or 1719, James L. Tort established a trading post on a small stream near a spring on the southern edge of what is now Carlisle. The trading post lasted for about ten years.

CUMBERLAND COUNTY - In the latter part of June, 1863, Confederate troops on their way to Gettysburg, reached Carlisle and camped just outside the town. On July 1st, after hearing that the battle had started at Gettysburg, the Confederate troops burned the U.S. Army barracks and headed for Gettysburg.

CUMBERLAND COUNTY - Fort Lowther was established about 1753 with five dwellings nearby. It was an important frontier outpost. The fort was also known as Carlisle's Fort and later became the town of Carlisle.

CUMBERLAND COUNTY - Several Indian villages were located within this county. The Carlisle Historical Society should have information on the location of these villages.

DAUPHIN COUNTY - Several good places to search in this county are located along the canals. Old buildings, piers and landings are still visible. The canals were as follows: The Union Canal, built in 1811, and passing through Dauphin County, following the Swatars Creek for twenty miles and entering the State Canal at Portsmouth on the Susquehanna; the Pennsylvania Canal enters from the southern extremity of Dauphin County and runs to Duncan's Island, ten miles above Harrisburg; The Wisonisco Canal, built in 1842, extended from Clark's Ferry to Millersburg, a distance ot twelve miles.

DAUPHIN COUNTY - Peixtan, an Indian village in the early 1700's was located near where Harrisburg is today.

DAUPHIN COUNTY - Fort Everitt, a small stockade, was built in the early 1750's, for protection of the settlers from Indians.

DAUPHIN COUNTY - Barnett's Fort was built in 1756 about one and one-half mile from where Linglestown is today. The fort was a frontier refuge in 1763.

DAUPHIN COUNTY - Fort Halifax was about one-half mile from where Halifax stands today. It was built in 1756 and used during the French and Indian War.

DAUPHIN COUNTY - Fort Hunter was built about one-half mile from the Rockville Bridge on U.S.22. It was a stockaded blockhouse, erected in 1755 and abandoned after 1763 and fell into ruins.

DAUPHIN COUNTY - Near Manada Gap was the log house fort built by James Brown and named Fort Manada. The fort was used from January 1756 until May 1757, with about 21 officers and men stationed here.

DAUPHIN COUNTY - Camp George Gordon Meade was about one-half mile from where Middletown is today. The camp covered three square miles and was used during the Spanish-American War.

DAUPHIN COUNTY - Patton's Fort was about one mile west of Linglestown. It was a station of the Paxton Rangers and was used from 1756 until 1763.

DAUPHIN COUNTY - Fort Swatora was built in the 1750's, and was used during the French and Indian War.

DAUPHIN COUNTY - The small village of Coxtown, now almost gone, at one time had a church, school, two taverns and about 20 homes.

DAUPHIN COUNTY - Franklin, no longer on the maps, had a tavern and several houses at one time.

DAUPHIN COUNTY - Ask in Harrisburg for directions to Clarks Ferry, a near-ghost town, it is no longer listed as a postoffice.

DELAWARE COUNTY - The Battle of Brandywine, near where Chadds Ford is today, occured on September II, 1777, between about 11,000 American patriots led by George Washington and 18,000 British and Hessian troops under Howe. The Americans were defeated. General Lafayette was wounded during this battle but would not leave his post.

DELAWARE COUNTY - Check at Media for the locations of Pointers, the post office has been discontinued and it is no longer on the map, and Chadds Ford that was the center of the Battle of the Brandywine.

ELK COUNTY - Indian "forts" are located on a ridge east of Russell City. There are 33 known Indian village sites in Elk County. Several hundred yards upstream from the mouth of Bear Creek is a spring where the Indians obtained war paint (iron oxide). A village was close by. The Historical Society in Ridgeway can give more information on the location of these Indian villages.

ELK COUNTY - Benzinger, a ghost lumber camp, had a mill, company stores, boarding house and about twelve homes. Now all are gone.

ELK COUNTY - Dent's Run, a near-ghost town, was a saw mill and coal town with several houses. There is very little left today.

ELK COUNTY - Loleta was once a busy lumber camp with a two room school, large sawmill, stables, a store and several hundred people. But like most of the early lumber camps, when the trees were gone, the town also died.

ELK COUNTY - Glen Hazel, a near ghost town, had saw mills, tannery and twenty or thirty houses at one time. The saw mills and tannery are gone today along with many of the houses.

ELK COUNTY - Hallton has only a few houses left. At one time it had saw mills and a chemical company.

ELK COUNTY - Horton City lasted only about six years before it became a ghost town. There were lumber mills coal mining and brick yards. These are all now gone.

ELK COUNTY - Straight is today a ghost town. At one time there were saw mills, general store, feed store, pool room, church, school, depot, chemical plant and houses. Nothing is left today.

ELK COUNTY - Instanter, today is a ghost town, at one time had a saw mill and tannery.

ELK COUNTY - Nansen, a lumber ghost town, had a chemical plant along with the usual saw mills. Both are now gone.

ELK COUNTY - Portland City, a near-ghost town, had saw mills, kindling factory and tannery, all now gone.

ELK COUNTY - Rainstown, today nothing but open fields, had lumber mills and several houses for their workers.

ELK COUNTY - Wilmere is a ghost town today and it had both coal mines and lumber mills.

ELK COUNTY - Wilcox had a tannery, saw mill and chemical plant. All gone now.

ERIE COUNTY - In Waterford is the site where Fort Le Boeuf stood. Three different forts have been at this site. The French were first from 1753 until 1759. In 1760, the English rebuilt the falling down fort and used it until 1763 when Indians burned it. Then American settlers built the last fort in 1794 to protect themselves from the Indians.

ERIE COUNTY - At Platea can be seen ruins of the old channel of the Erie Extension Canal. There were 28 locks within a two mile stretch, used in lowering boats headed for Lake Erie. The canal was in use from 1844 until 1871.

ERIE COUNTY - Near Asbury Chapel can still be seen remains of the Erie Extension Canal, running from New Castle to Erie.

ERIE COUNTY - Inquire in Erie for Hammett and Lowville, two dying towns that are no longer listed as having postoffices.

FAYETTE COUNTY - Near Masontown was Provance Settlement, a favorite stopping point for men going to Fort Pitt in the 1770's

FAYETTE COUNTY - Close to the junction of the Cheat River and the Monongahela was Ice's Ford, a small settlement during the 1770's. For many years it was one of the last stopping points for men heading into western Pennsylvania and the Ohio country.

FAYETTE COUNTY - About five miles from Uniontown was one of the six original toll houses on the Cumberland or National Road. The house was built in 1835.

FAYETTE COUNTY - Near Perryopolis are the ruins of a grist mill built on the order of George Washington, who owned the land in 1774.

FAYETTE COUNTY - Dunbar's Camp, where Colonel Dunbar and his detachment following General Braddock with his heavy baggage, made their last camp in June of 1755. When Braddock was defeated, Dunbar destroyed all the supplies he was carrying and fled.

FAYETTE COUNTY - Near Connellsville is the site where Christopher Gist settled in 1753. In 1754, Indians drove him out and destroyed the plantation.

FAYETTE COUNTY - At Brownsville is the site of what has been called Redstone Old Fort or Fort Burd. In 1754 the Ohio Company had a storehouse here.

FAYETTE COUNTY - Fort Gaddis was built about two miles south of where Uniontown is today, in 1764.

FAYETTE COUNTY - Fort Mason was built as a blockhouse in 1774 and was used during the Revolutionary War.

FAYETTE COUNTY - Fort Necessity was begun by George Washington on May 29, 1754, and he and his men were driven out by the French on July 4th, 1754.

FAYETTE COUNTY - Alliance Furnace, the first iron furnace west of the Alleghenies was built one mile from Dawson in 1779. The ruins are still visible.

FAYETTE COUNTY - Center Furnace, also called Dunbar Furnace was built in 1815 and was used until 1830 Remains of the stack base, mill race and stone foundations are still visible.

FAYETTE COUNTY - Coolspring Furnace was east of Uniontown, built before 1820, and used until 1860. Part of the stack, mill race and slag pile are still there.

FAYETTE COUNTY - Fairfield Furnace was built on Georges Creek, northeast of Fairchance, in 1792 and was used until 1870. Nothing remains today.

FAYETTE COUNTY - The Fayette Furnace, southeast

of Normalville was also known as Bucks Run and Rogers Mill. It was erected in 1815 and was discontinued in 1840.

FAYETTE COUNTY - Indian Creek had several saw mills, about 25 homes and a store. Now all this is gone and the area is deserted.

FAYETTE COUNTY - Laurel Furnace was once an iron ore center, later had a saw mill. The saw mill closed in 1906 and the area became deserted.

FAYETTE COUNTY - The Mary Ann Furnace was built on Mountain Creek east of Haydenton about 1800 and was used until 1840. The ruins of the stack are still visible.

FAYETTE COUNTY - The Mount Vernon Furnace was built near Wooddale between 1795 and 1800 and was discontinued in 1830.

FAYETTE COUNTY - The St. Johns Furnace on Indian Creek was built in 1807 and used until 1828. Part of the stack is still standing.

FAYETTE COUNTY - Union Furnace #1 and #2 are south of Connellsville, on Dunbar Creek. #1 was built in 1791 and replaced by #2 (a larger one) in 1793. #2 was built just across the creek and downstream from #1. Part of the stack of #1 is still standing, but nothing remains of #2.

FAYETTE COUNTY - Ohiopyle, on the Youghiogheny River, is a near-ghost town today. The saw mills closed in the early 1920's.

FAYETTE COUNTY - Bruner Run, a ghost town today, had a company store, saw mill, boarding house and several homes. The town lasted only about five years, until the lumber was all out.

FORREST COUNTY - An Indian village known as "Lower Town" was located on the opposite side of the river from where Tionesta is today.

FOREST COUNTY - Not far from Tionesta is the extinct village of Kellettville, which was razed to make way for the Tionesta flood control dam. Once it boasted a high school, post office a dozen thriving businesses and about 1200 people. It was a flourishing lumbering town, and there are still many alive who can recall watching a Memorial or 4th of July parade in Kellettville. Only 16 permanent residents reside in the area, which is now a part of history. It could be a bottle digger's paradise as well as a good spot for coinshooters.

FOREST COUNTY - Across the river from East Hickory is the site where the Indian village known as "Upper Town" was located in 1767.

FOREST COUNTY - About two miles south of East Hickory was "Middle Town", an Indian village in the 1760's. Several Indian paths from the south ended here.

FOREST COUNTY - Data can be obtained at Tionesta on the location of East Hickory, a near-ghost town.

FRANKLIN COUNTY - On June 30, 1863, Confederate and Union forces had a skirmish near Greencastle.

FRANKIN COUNTY - On July 29, 1864, Confederate troops marched north and reached Chambersburg. The next morning they burned the town and moved on to McConnellsburg. The town of Chambersburg saw action several times during the Civil War. The first was when "Jeb" Stuart raided the area in 1862. In 1863 the Confederate forces occupied the town for a short time and General Lee made his headquarters on the outskirts.

FRANKLIN COUNTY - Fort Chambers was built in 1756, as a stockade surrounding the house and mill. It was fortified by a cannon.

FRANKLIN COUNTY - About a mile west of Welch Run is the site of Fort Davis, built in 1755, and used for several years.

FRANKLIN COUNTY - Fort Loudon was built in 1756 by

the Provincial Government. In 1763 Colonists forces forced the withdrawal of a British Garrison from the fort.

FRANKLIN COUNTY - North of Edenville is where Fort McCord was built. On April 1, 1756, Indians burned the fort and killed or captured 27 people.

FRANKLIN COUNTY - Fort Marshall was built about 1755, five miles south of where Mercersburg is today. It was used as a station in the daily military patrol to guard the southwestern frontier from raids during the French and Indian War.

FRANKLIN COUNTY - Fort McDowell was built near Markes in 1755 and was also used by Provincial authorities for a year.

FRANKLIN COUNTY - Just west of St. James is where Fort Wadell was built in 1755 for refuge of the settlers from Indians.

FRANKLIN COUNTY - Two miles southeast of Mercersburg was the location of Rev. Steels Fort. He stockaded his church in 1755 for the use of settlers in the area.

FRANKLIN COUNTY - The village of Upton, no longer on the map, at one time had a few houses, store and tavern. It was located between Waynesboro and McConnellstown.

FULTON COUNTY - Fort Lyttleton was begun in 1755 and was garrisoned by Provincial and regular troops. By 1764 it had fallen into ruins.

FULTON COUNTY - On June 24th and again on June 29 1863, the Union and Confederated met at McConnellsburg in brief skirmishes.

FULTON COUNTY - Inquire at McConnellsburg for directions to Burnt Cabins and Fort Littleton, both near-ghost towns.

GREENE COUNTY - East of the town of Garads Fort is the site of the original fort, built in 1777 and used until sometime in the 1780's.

GREENE COUNTY - In Wind Ridge was the Ryerson's Blockhouse, built in 1792, during the state's last trouble with the Indians.

GREENE COUNTY - From 1805 until 1849, the first glass factory west of the Monongahela was in operation near what is now Greensboro. The building has fallen into ruins.

GREENE COUNTY - South of Dry Tavern is where Fort Swan was built in 1774 and used during the Revolutionary War.

GREENE COUNTY - Fort Jackson was built in 1774 as a stockaded cabin, and later became a palisaded fort containing several cabins of settlers. The town of Waynesburg grew from this fort.

HUNTINGDON COUNTY - Near Spruce Creek are the sites of two forges built in 1805 and 1809 and used until 1850. Only the ruins are visible.

HUNTINGDON COUNTY - About one-fourth mile east of Huntingdon is the site of Fort Standing Stone, an important outpost of the area.

HUNTINGDON COUNTY - McAlevys Fort, built in 1778, was a frontier blockhouse that served as an early refuge for settlers in the area against Indians.

HUNTINGDON COUNTY - Fort Shirley was built in 1755 near where Shirleysburg is today. At first it was only a stockade but later it was enlarged and became a major fort in the area.

HUNTINGDON COUNTY - Outside of Arbisonia can be found ruins of many charcoal iron furnaces and forges built and used between 1790 and 1850.

HUNTINGDON COUNTY - Mill Creek was the site of pre-Revolutionary grist and saw mills, and later became an iron center when Mill Creek Furnace was built in 1838. Ruins of this furnaces, grist and saw mills and the canal can all still be found.

HUNTINGDON COUNTY - Information can be obtained at Huntingdon on the locations of Franklinsville, Spruce Creek, Shade Gap and Water Street, all near-ghost towns. Franklinville and Water Street no longer have postoffices.

INDIANA COUNTY - About a mile west of Indiana is where Moorhead's Fort was built about 1781 and used for several years.

INDIANA COUNTY - The small village of Armagh, a near-ghost town, was a noted stage stop. During stagecoach days it had more taverns than it has houses today.

INDIANA COUNTY - The small town of Nola once had a stage stop, tavern and postoffice, now all gone.

INDIANA COUNTY - All that is left of Graceton are abandoned coke ovens and some dilapidated company houses, of a once busy coal camp.

INDIANA COUNTY - The County Clerk at Indiana can help with directions to Coral and Josephine, now ghost towns.

JEFFERSON COUNTY - A coal mining town called Canifer at one time had several hundred people living there. Now there are only about six houses.

JEFFERSON COUNTY   Ask at Brookville for the location of Fuller, a ghost town of which nothing is left.

JUNIATA COUNTY - Northwest of Mexico is the location of Fort Bigham, built in 1754 and destroyed by Indians in 1756.

JUNIATA COUNTY - East of Mexico is the site of

Patterson's Fort, built in 1755 and used for several years for protection of the settlers against Indians.

JUNIATA COUNTY - Mexico, a near-ghost town, is a small village that at one time had several industrial plants. The last one closed in 1938. Now it is mainly a farm community with several old stone houses still there.

LACKAWANNA COUNTY - Near West Scranton is where the Indian village under Chief Capoose was settled in 1743.

LACKAWANNA COUNTY - Lake Ariel, an abandoned amusement park is located about twenty miles east of Scranton, on route #191. The park closed in the early 1900's, and many coins and artifacts from the turn of the century could possibly be found.

LACKAWANNA COUNTY - The small village of Thornhurst is slowly becoming a ghost town, the postoffice has been discontinued.

LANCASTER COUNTY - East of Columbia was the location of Wright's Ferry, founded in 1726, on the Susquehanna River. It was an early center for turnpike, canal and railroad traffic.

LANCASTER COUNTY - About a mile south of Brainbridge is where the Conoy Indian tribe had a settlement from 1718 until 1743.

LANCASTER COUNTY - On Harmon Creek near Brickersville can be found ruins of the forge dams that supplied water for the Upper and Lower Hopewell Forges. Several houses were in the area for the workers.

LANCASTER COUNTY - Between Washington and Millersville was where the Conestoga Indian town stood. William Penn Visited this village in 1701. In 1763, the Indians were massacred by a frontier mob called the "Paxtang Boys".

LANCASTER COUNTY - In 1789, the Susquehanna settlement of Peach Bottom was considered as a site for the national capital. When it was not chosen it gradually fell into decay and was reclaimed by the wilderness.

LANCASTER COUNTY - Oregon, a near-ghost town, as early as 1775 had a stage stop at the Oregon Inn. The postoffice has been closed for several years.

LANCASTER COUNTY - The County Clerk at Lancaster can be of help in locating these near-ghost towns: Wakefield, White Horse and Smoketown. Wakefield and White Horse no longer have postoffices.

LAWRENCE COUNTY - South of New Castle is the location of Kushushies Towns, a group of Indian villages in the area. The towns were abandoned after the Revolutionary War.

LAWRENCE COUNTY - Information can be obtained at New Castle on Harlansburg, no longer listed with a postoffice.

LEBANON COUNTY - Near Myerstown are the remains of one of the locks of the Union Canal, used from 1828 until 1884.

LEBANON COUNTY - Reed's Fort was built in 1755, northeast of Harrisburg, near the Dauphin County Line.

LEBANON COUNTY - Two miles north of Lickdale is where Fort Swatara was built to guard the gap in Blue Mountain. Indians used the gap to raid frontier settlements during the French and Indian War.

LEBANON COUNTY - About four miles northwest of Lickdale are a dam, guard lock and several lift lock remains of the Union Canal.

LEBANON COUNTY - In Newmonton is the site of Fort Zeller, built in 1723 and rebuilt in 1745. It was used as a place of refuge during the Indian Wars.

LEBANON COUNTY - Ask in Lebanon for directions to

Miners Village, Mt., Gretna and Colebrook, all near ghost towns. The postoffices have all been closed.

LEHIGH COUNTY - South of Egypt was the site of Fort Deshler, a stone fort built in 1760. By 1940 the fort had all but disappeared.

LEHIGH COUNTY - East of Lynnport was a blockhouse built about 1756, and called Fort Everett. Troops were stationed here to protect the settlers during the French and Indian War.

LEHIGH COUNTY - Check with the County Clerk at Allentown for directions to Shimmertown, no longer listed as a postoffice.

LUZERNE COUNTY - The Indian village of Misheheckon was located near where present day Nesopeck stands.

LUZERNE COUNTY - Near West Pittston, below Campbells Ledge, was the Indian village of Assarughney. The Delaware Indians occupied this village after 1737.

LUZERNE COUNTY - Jenkins Fort was built near where West Pittston is today, in 1776. The British captured the fort on July 1, 1778, and burned it.

LUZERNE COUNTY - Near the mouth of Wapwallopen Creek was the Indian village of Wapwallopen. The village was on the "Warriors Path", and was visited by many different tribes.

LUZERNE COUNTY - Near Wyoming, on July 3, 1778, 300 American patriots under Colonel Zebulon Butler were defeated by 1,100 British, Tories and Indians led by Major John Butler. The captives were massacred, the survivors who managed to escape, fled to Forty Fort, a few miles away.

LUZERNE COUNTY - The Sugarloaf Massacre took place about five miles northwest of Hazelton on September II, 1780. A group of Tories and Indians surprised a detachment of Northumberland County militia and massacred all of them.

LUZERNE COUNTY - In May 1769, a large party of Yankees from Connecticut led by Major John Durkee built Fort Durkee at Wyoming. In June a company of Pennsylvania militia were sent to run the Yankees away. This attempt failed. A second battle occured in 1771, and the third attempt was in 1783-84. These battles have been called the Pennymite Wars, for the control of the Wyoming Valley of Pennsylvania.

LUZERNE COUNTY - Data can be obtained at Wilkes-Barre on Bear Creek and Stoddardsville, near-ghost towns.

LYCOMING COUNTY - Near Jersey Shore is the site of Fort Antes, built in 1776. Indians later burned the fort after finding it abandoned during the Great Runaway of white settlers from the Wyoming Valley.

LYCOMING COUNTY - Just north of Muncy Fort Munsy was built in 1778. The British and Indians destroyed it in 1779.

LYCOMING COUNTY - Northeast of Muncy several grist mills stood. The first one was built about 1772 and was burned by the Indians in 1779. Other mills were built in 1783 and 1800. The last mill was discontinued after 1872.

LYCOMING COUNTY - North of Muncy can be found the ruins of the West Branch Division of the Pennsylvania Canal. About 1400 feet of vertical wall 22 feet high supported the towpath.

LYCOMING COUNTY - Up Mills Run, off Pine Creek, can still be seen the remains of an old railroad built during the lumbering days.

LYCOMING COUNTY - Along the water front in Williamsport, during the period of 1860-1900, many saw mills operated. Most of them are gone today.

LYCOMING COUNTY - Asaph, once a busy little town, is today a near-ghost town. At one time there was a saw mill, blacksmith shop, boarding house, postoffice and store. Now there are only a few houses remaining.

LYCOMING COUNTY - About two miles from the mouth of Pine Creek is Furnace Run, a logging camp. A railroad and saw mill were located on this small creek. The railroad and mill closed about 1916.

LYCOMING COUNTY - Slate Run, today a near-ghost town, at one time had a saw mill with a railroad built in 1885. There were three hotels, post office, stores and houses. The mill closed in 1910. Today only a store and a few houses are left.

LYCOMING COUNTY - Inquire at Montourville for directions to Bodine, a near-ghost town.

MCKEAN COUNTY - Seneca Springs, south of Kane, was a stopping place on an old Indian trail leading from Onandaga, New York, to the Ohio and Carolina region.

MCKEAN COUNTY - Near Bradford is the ghost town of Hazelton Mills, at one time a thriving village. Today only a few buildings are left.

MCKEAN COUNTY - Sergeant, today a near-ghost town, had a chemical plant and several houses at one time. The plant is now gone.

MCKEAN COUNTY - Quinnwood, a lumber ghost town had two saw mills and several houses, now all gone.

MCKEAN COUNTY - Betula and Nowich, twin ghost towns, today leave no trace of where they were. At one time both were thriving lumber towns.

MCKEAN COUNTY - Beyond the village of Clermont there was once a socialistic community known as Teutonia. The village, along with Ginalsburg, is said to have been established by Paltinate Germans. The two communities lasted less than six years and were gone by the time the Civil War started. Faint evidence of their existence remains.

MERCER COUNTY - Southeast of West Middlesex was the Indian village of Shenanga Town, used by Indians from 1750 until 1785. A few bands remained in the area until about 1812.

MERCER COUNTY - The only remaining canal lock in the county still standing on the Erie Extension Canal, is located east of Sharpsville.

MERCER COUNTY - East of Clark is the location of Pymatuning, a Delaware Indian village from 1764-1785.

MERCER COUNTY - The Clay Furnace, named for Henry Clay, was located west of Charleston in 1845. The furnace was abandoned in 1861.

MERCER COUNTY - Johnson's Tavern, located on U.S. Route 19, about a mile north of Leesburg, was a tavern during stagecoach travel. Originally built in 1831 by Arthur Johnston, who had immigrated from Ireland earlier. The stone structure served as a stopping place for stagecoach passengers traveling on the Pittsburgh-Mercer Road, and it stood conviently near Springfield Furnace, which was in operation after 1837. Johnston operated this tavern until 1842.

MERCER COUNTY - The County Clerk at Mercer can help you locate Sheakleyville, a near-ghost town.

MIFFLIN COUNTY - Southwest of Lewistown, along the streams can be found the ruins of many charcoal iron furnaces and forges built between 1790 and 1850.

MIFFLIN COUNTY - Southwest of Lewistown is the site of Fort Granville, built in 1755. The French and Indians destroyed it in 1756.

MIFFLIN COUNTY - Southwest of Lewistown are the stonework and old bed of three locks of the Pennsylvania Canal.

MIFFLIN COUNTY - Check at Lewistown for directions to Alfarata, not even the postoffice is left.

MONROE COUNTY - Fort Depuy was built in 1755 and used for several years as protection against the Indians It was located near where Shawnee is today.

MONROE COUNTY - Fort Hyndshaw was built in 1755, it was a 70 foot square fort along Bashkill Creek. The fort was used during the French and Indian War.

MONROE COUNTY - Fort Hamilton was built in 1756, near where Stroudsburg is today, and was an 80 foot square stockade with 41 men stationed there. It was abandoned in 1757.

MONROE COUNTY - Near Tannersvills is the site where Learned's Tavern stood in the 1770's. On June 19, 1779, General Sullivan and his troops camped here on their way to Wyoming to attack the Indians in the upper Susquehanna River area.

MONROE COUNTY - During the last week of May and the first week of June in 1779, General Sullivan and his army camped at "Hungry Hill", before crossing over the Pocono Mountains.

MONROE COUNTY - The Dansbury Mission was erected about 1744 by the Moravian missionaries. The Indians destroyed the mission in 1755 and it was not rebuilt.

MONROE COUNTY - About a mile from Kresgeville was the site of Fort Norris, built in 1756 and used for several years.

MONROE COUNTY - Ask for directions at Stroudsburg to Blakeslee Corners, a near-ghost town.

MONTGOMERY COUNTY - On December 13-19, 1777, the Continental Army camped near Gulph Mills on their way to Valley Forge.

MONTGOMERY COUNTY - Betzwood, where early motion picture experimental work was done, is slowly dying. All that remains of the studios are small vaults, resembling old springhouses, used to store the celluloid in.

MONTOUR COUNTY - Fort Bosley was built near where Washingtonville is today, in the 1770's. In 1777 a small force was garrisoned there to protect the settlers from the Indians. A grist mill was located here and used for several years.

NORTHAMPTON COUNTY - South of Raubsville can be seen the bed of the Delaware Canal, which ran parallel to the Delaware River.

NORTHAMPTON COUNTY - Near Northampton is the site of the Indian town of Hackendanqua.

NORTHAMPTON COUNTY - The County Clerk at Easton can give you information on several abandoned iron mines in the Raubsville area. Evidence of these mines and former villages can still be seen.

NORTHAMPTON COUNTY - An old Indian village called Nain was located near where old Bethlehem is today. By 1760 the Indians had left the area.

NORTHAMPTON COUNTY - Inquire at Easton for the village of Slateford, no longer listed in postal records.

NORTHUMBERLAND COUNTY - Mahoning, an Indian village was located about a mile below where Danville is today, on Mahoning Creek, just inside the county line.

NORTHUMBERLAND COUNTY - About halfway between Northumberland and Danville was the location of an Indian village called NIshmekkachio.

NORTHUMBERLAND COUNTY - Fort Boone was located near the mouth of Muddy Run during the 1770's. The fort was named for Hawkins Boone, a colonial captain who helped build and defend the fort.

NORTHUMBERLAND COUNTY - Fort Brady was built as a stockaded house in 1777, near where Muncy is today. In 1779 Indians destroyed the fort.

NORTHUMBERLAND COUNTY - Fort McMahon was built near the present town of Pottsgrove. Nothing remains of the fort today.

NORTHUMBERLAND COUNTY - About five miles from Milton is the site of Fort Freland, a stockaded house, built in 1778. On June 29, 1779, the British and Indians captured the fort, taking prisoner or killing all of the 21 men garrisoned there.

NORTHUMBERLAND COUNTY - Fort Menninger was located on the north bank of White Deer Creek. A mill was also located there. The fort was burned by the Indians in July of 1779.

NORTHUMBERLAND COUNTY - Fort Montgomery was located in Paradise Valley about 1777. It was destroyed by the Indians in 1779, during the Great Runaway.

NORTHUMBERLAND COUNTY - Fort Reid was built in 1777, near where Lock Haven is tody. During the Great Runaway in 1778-79, the fort was deserted and never used again.

NORTHUMBERLAND COUNTY - One mile above Milton is the site where Fort Swartz was built in the late 1770's. The fort was never attacked by Indians, but many settlers gathered there during Indian scares.

NORTHUMBERLAND COUNTY - In 1772, Henry Antes built a grist mill on Antes Creek. In 1777 he erected a stockade near the mill, covering one-half acre. In 1779 Indians attacked the fort and set it on fire. The large logs smoldered and went out. Later the fort fell into decay and nothing remains today.

NORTHUMBERLAND COUNTY - Near Northumberland can still be seen traces of the tow path and the canal bed of the Pennsylvania Canal, built in 1829-32 and used until 1901.

NORTHUMBERLAND COUNTY - Data may be obtained at Dunbury on Pacinos, Weigh Scales and Fishers Ferry, all small hamlets becoming ghost towns today. None of them are listed as having postoffices.

PERRY COUNTY – About a mile west of Laysville was the site of Fort Robinson, built in 1755 and used for several years.

PERRY COUNTY – Traces of the Pennsylvania Canal (Susquehanna Division) can still be seen north of Amity Hall.

PERRY COUNTY – The little village of Millerstown had 17 inns during the period the canals were being built. Several of these old houses are still standing. After the canals were discontinued the town began to lose both people and businesses.

PERRY COUNTY – Amith Hall, little more than a truck stop today, is littered with ruins of the canals which intersected here. The postoffice already has been closed.

PERRY COUNTY – The small village of Andersonville once had a tavern, store and church, today little is left.

PIKE COUNTY – North of Lackawaxen was where the battle of Minisink took place on July 22, 1779. Over 175 settlers attacked 300 Tories and Indians led by Chief Joseph Brant of the Mohawks. All but 25 of the settlers were killed.

PIKE COUNTY – Stockport is now a ghost town with some of the old buildings still standing. The school, blacksmith shop and church are still there along with some of the original homes. The town was settled in the 1700's and thrived until the mid 1800's.

PIKE COUNTY – All that is left of Stockport, near Lackawaxen, are a few old buildings, parts of grist mill and a few foundation stones. At one time there was a school, general store, blacksmith shop and a factory. Numerous artifacts have been found. The area is now private property, so be sure to obtain permission to search.

POTTER COUNTY – Roulette was once a booming lumber town, now has many deserted houses as the lumber was all gone by 1912 and the people have moved on.

POTTER COUNTY - Atop the famous Allegheny River portage at Keating Summit, is the ghost town of Gardeau, which was a thriving lumber town with one of the largest spas in Pennsylvania. Hundreds of the affluent came to Noah Parker's resort to take the mineral baths and drink the foul smelling water.

An old brick chimney is all that remains of the famous inn, and the brick outbuildings in the rear are now a pile of rubble covered by day lilies, wild grapes and mullien. The deserted village and the area surrounding the old hotel should be a coinshooter's paradise. Think of the number of bottles that found their way into Parker's dump, which has never been found.

POTTER COUNTY - Blowville, near Bailey Brook, was once a thriving community with hotels, stores, bordellos, and prosperous business establishments in the 1890's. Not one sign of the village remains today.

POTTER COUNTY - Near Coudersport on State#872, are the remains of Austin Dam, that gave way in 1911 and demolished the town of Austin, killing 87 people. The town rebuilt a short distance away from the original site.

POTTER COUNTY - The village of Oleona, once a busy little village, today does not appear on maps and no longer has a postoffice.

POTTER COUNTY - The village of Sweden Valley is slowly becoming nothing more than a crossroads farming hamlet. The postoffice is closed.

POTTER COUNTY - About 1910, a chemical plant was built at what was known as Lyman Run. About twenty-five houses were built for the workers. The plant only operated for about seven years. Nothing is left today.

POTTER COUNTY - Cross Fork saw her mills destroyed by fire twice, and rebuilt each time. There were hotels, saloons, school and newspaper. In 1894 the population was about 1,500. By 1920 most of the buildings had disappeared and the mills closed.

POTTER COUNTY - The lumber camps of Costello and Galeton lasted only a few years and then they became ghost towns.

POTTER COUNTY - Germania once had a brewery and was quite a thriving town. Today very little is left of the village and the brewery is gone.

POTTER COUNTY - Hulls was also known as Conerad, and at once time was a busy town with a huge saw mill. Very little remains of the town today.

POTTER COUNTY - Keating Summit, a lumber ghost town, had several company homes, a boarding house along with the customary saw mill. All is now gone.

POTTER COUNTY - Mine, today a ghost town, is located a few miles west of Coudersport. At one time the village had at least 1,200 people living there. It was a busy lumber town with hotels, stores, restaurants, school and postoffice. Very little remains today except the old depot, which is falling down.

POTTER COUNTY - Walton had a chemical plant, hotel, post office (called Gaffney) and a few houses. The plant closed in early 1920's, and little remains today.

POTTER COUNTY - Check with the County Clerk at Coudersport for the location of Osborne and Francis, two abandoned lumber camps.

SCHUYLKILL COUNTY - Fort Franklin was built in 1756 near where Snyders is tday. The fort was abandoned in 1757 because of Indians.

SCHUYLKILL COUNTY - Fort Franklin, later called Fort William, was built near where Auburn is today. The fort was erected in 1755 and was used for several years.

SNYDER COUNTY - Near Kreamer was the Schoch Blockhouse, built about 1770 and used until 1783.

SNYDER COUNTY - Information can be obtained in

Middlesbury for directions to Salem, a near-ghost town. The postoffice has been closed.

SOMERSET COUNTY - A Civilian Conservation Corps (called CCC) Camp was located about two miles from Salisbury during 1934-38. Several hundred men were stationed here during that period. The site is now called Mt. Davis Recreation Park.

SOMERSET COUNTY - East of Stoyestown was the Stoney Creek Encampment, established in 1758. This was a fortified supply depot on the Forbes Road.

SOMERSET COUNTY - Near Confluence are mounds that are believed to have been used by Indians for burial. A large village stood here as early as 1700.

SOMERSET COUNTY - Fort Dewart, one of Forbes forts on his campaign to take Fort Duquesne in 1758, was located on top of Allegheny Hill, near the Bedford County line.

SOMERSET COUNTY - Northeast of Ursina are the remains of two palasided Indian villages with extensive house and burial remains. These villages date from the Recovery Period.

SOMERSET COUNTY - Arrow, now a ghost town, was a lumber camp for several years and at one time had a kindling wood factory.

SOMERSET COUNTY - In the busy little town of Ashtola there was a postoffice, company store, saw mill, boarding house, blacksmith shop, school and about sixty houses. Later it became knowr as Old Ashtola when New Ashtola located about three miles away. Old Ashtola no longer appears on the map.

SOMERSET COUNTY - Glenco, now a ghost town, had a saw mill with a boarding house for the workers. All now gone.

SOMERSET COUNTY - Humbolt had several coal mines

and saw mills. At one time there were over one hundred company houses for workers, a hotel and stores. Today most of these are gone.

SOMERSET COUNTY - McClintock Run, now a ghost town had a saw mill, blacksmith shop, store, boarding house and several homes. Nothing is left there today.

SOMERSET COUNTY - Roddy was a lumber camp with a boarding house and a saw mill, now all gone.

SOMERSET COUNTY - The ghost town of Seanor had a saw mill built about 1886 and coal was discovered in 1896. Today very little is left of the village.

SOMERSET COUNTY - Unamis, a logging ghost town in the southern part of the county, had the usual boarding house, company store, mills and a coal mine. Today it is all gone.

SOMERSET COUNTY - Ask at Somerset for directions to Addison, Somerfield and Jennerstown, all slowly dying towns.

SULLIVAN COUNTY - Near Forksville was an old woolen factory that made cloth for the army during the War of 1812. A flood in 1816 destroyed the factory.

SULLIVAN COUNTY - Ricketts had houses, hotel, store, saw mill and a postoffice. Today there are no buildings left to show where this ghost town stood.

SULLIVAN COUNTY Sonesville, a lumber ghost town on Kettle Creek, at one time had a school, mill and a boarding house. By 1922 the town had almost completely disappeared.

SULLIVAN COUNTY - Masten was another ghost town. At one time there were about 90 houses, store, hotel, boarding house, barber shop and pool room. The town began to die in the 1930's, when the timber was all cut and by 1941 had become deserted.

SUSQUEHANNA COUNTY - On the Susquehanna River, near where Salt Lick Creek empties into it, was an old Tuscaroa Indian village.

SUSQUEHANNA COUNTY - The County Clerk at Montrose can help you with the location of Lenox. It no longer has a postoffice.

TIOGA COUNTY - Leetonia, a lumber ghost town, had stores, postoffice, saw mill, tannery, school and severa houses. The mill closed in 1921 and the people began moving away.

TIOGA COUNTY - Leolyn, an abandoned 2½ story brick house, built in 1830, is now falling into ruins. It was known as the Halfway Tavern and was used for several years.

TIOGA COUNTY - Morris, a ghost town today, was once a coal and logging center. A chemical company had a small plant here. By 1928 most of the timber had been cut and very little is left of the town today.

TIOGA COUNTY - Tiadaghton has only a few houses left today of a once busy lumbering town. There was a hotel, two stores, postoffice, saw mills and twenty or thirty houses. The postoffice closed in 1936.

TIOGA COUNTY - Information can be obtained at Wellsboro on these former communities: Fall Brook, once a coal mining town, now has only one building left: Landrus was a mining and lumbering town, nothing left; Roaring Branch and Oregon Hill.

UNION COUNTY - Ask for directions at Lewisburg to Vicksburg, Harleton and McEwensville, all near-ghost towns today.

VENANGO COUNTY - Pithole, a ghost town that lasted only a year or two, was an oil boom town. It was established in 1865 and within a few months had over 15,000 population. There were banks, churches, hotels, postoffice, stores, saloons and a water system. All that remains are excavations and street lines.

VENANGO COUNTY - Kaneville was an oil boom town and at one time had over 1,000 people residing there. Today there are less than 100 and very little of the town remains.

VENANGO COUNTY - Inquire at Oil City for directions to Cherry Tree, Reno, and McClingockville, all near-ghost towns.

WARREN COUNTY - As early as 1749, an Indian village called Chauonyon was located where Warren is today. This was where the first of the lead plates M. Celoron de Bienville buried was placed. It claimed all the land along the Ohio for France. This plate was recovered by the Indians and taken to Col. William Johnston in New York. The area should have many Indian relics as the village was used for several years.

WARREN COUNTY - East of Irvine was the location of an Indian village of Buckalonns. Celoran visited here in 1749, when he was burying the lead plates on the Ohio River. The village was destroyed by Colonel Brodhead and his militia in 1779.

WASHINGTON COUNTY - West of West Middleton was where Doddridge's Fort was built about 1773, serving the area for several years.

WASHINGTON COUNTY - About three miles northwest of Claysville was the site of Miller's Blockhouse, built in 1780. The fort was successful in repelling an Indian attack in 1782.

WASHINGTON COUNTY - Rice's Fort was built in the early 1780's. near where Claysville is today. In 1782 Indians attacked the fort but were driven off.

WASHINGTON COUNTY - Wolff's Fort was built in 1780 near where Washington is today. It was one of the more important forts of the area and was used for several years.

WASHINGTON COUNTY - Hill Tavern, in operation since

1794, was a popular stop for stage coaches and waggoners for many years.

WASHINGTON COUNTY - Bane Town at one time had a postoffice, now closed, a store, blacksmith shop and about ten houses. Very little is left of this small town.

WASHINGTON COUNTY - Patterson's Mill no longer has a postoffice, at one time there was also a store, grist mill, church and school. These too are gone.

WASHINGTON COUNTY - Venice had a combination store and postoffice, blacksmith shop and about ten houses. All are gone.

WASHINGTON COUNTY - The County Clerk at Washington can help you locate Amity, Woodrow and Rea, all near-ghost towns.

WAYNE COUNTY - A large Indian village once stood at the junction of Equinuck Creek and the Delaware River. A trading post was located here for a short time during the 1750's.

WESTMORELAND COUNTY - On U.S. 22, east of Murrysville was the location of Washington Camp. This base for Forbes Road was built in November 1758, by Col. George Washington, "Commanding the Troops to ye Westward", on order of Col. Henry Boquet.

WESTMORELAND COUNTY - Near Ligonier was the Indian village of Loyalhanning, settled by the Delawares in 1727.

WESTMORELAND COUNTY - Eight miles east of Greensburg was the Dagworthy House built in 1758. It served as a hospital for men wounded in Grant's illfated Fort Duquesne raid. It was often called Grant's Paradise.

WESTMORELAND COUNTY - Southwest of Greensburg was Fort Allen, built in 1774. It was used during Dunmore's War and the Revolutionary War.

WESTMORELAND COUNTY - About seven miles east of Greensburg is where Twelve Mile Camp was set up by George Washington in 1758. In 1774, it was rebuilt and renamed Fort Shippen.

WESTMORELAND COUNTY - Inquire at Greensburg for the near-ghost town of North Washington.

WYOMING COUNTY - The Indian village of Wyalutimunk was located about two miles south of where Falls is today

WYOMING COUNTY - In Skinners Eddy, a near-ghost town, are cavernous warehouses, no longer used, along with deserted houses. The postoffice and stores are all gone.

WYOMING COUNTY - Clarkstown once had several grist mills and a post office, now all gone.

WYOMING COUNTY - Ricketts, a ghost lumber town, at one time had mills, a boarding house, stores and a cblacksmith shop. The last family left there in 1920. Today there is only one building left standing.

WYOMING COUNTY - Check at Tunkhannock for the location of Oslerhout and Falls, postoffices are both closed.

YORK COUNTY - About three miles east of York was the site of Camp Security, built in 1781. British prisoners of Burgoyne's army were held here, guarded by York Count malitia.

YORK COUNTY - South of Wrightsville can still be seen traces of the Susquehanna Canal.

YORK COUNTY - Cresap's Fort was built about 1730 near Craley. Cresap was evicted in 1736 by Penn agents who burned his fort. Cresap then went to Maryland and later on to Virginia.

YORK COUNTY - At Hanover, on June 30, 1863, Union and Confederate forces clashed with the Confederates, losing 135 men, wounded or missing and Union losses about 55. This was the first battle of the Civil War that was fought north of the Mason Dixon Line.

YORK COUNTY - Information can be obtained at York on Newberrytown and Strinestown, near-ghost towns that no longer have postoffices.

* * * * * * * * *

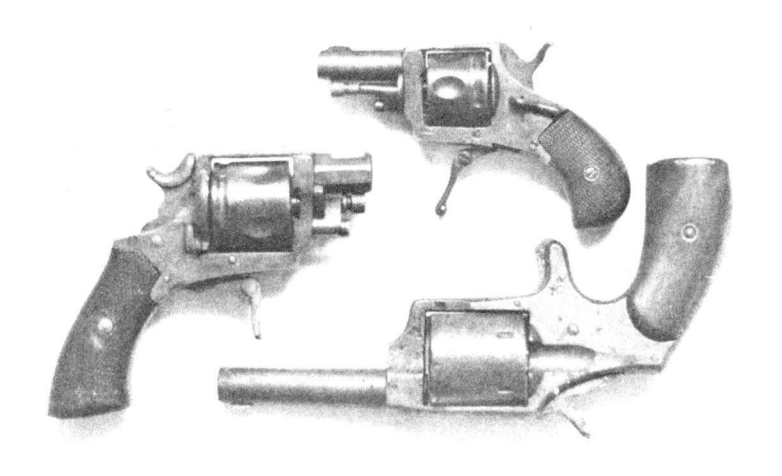

Some guns found by the author.

Indian signs

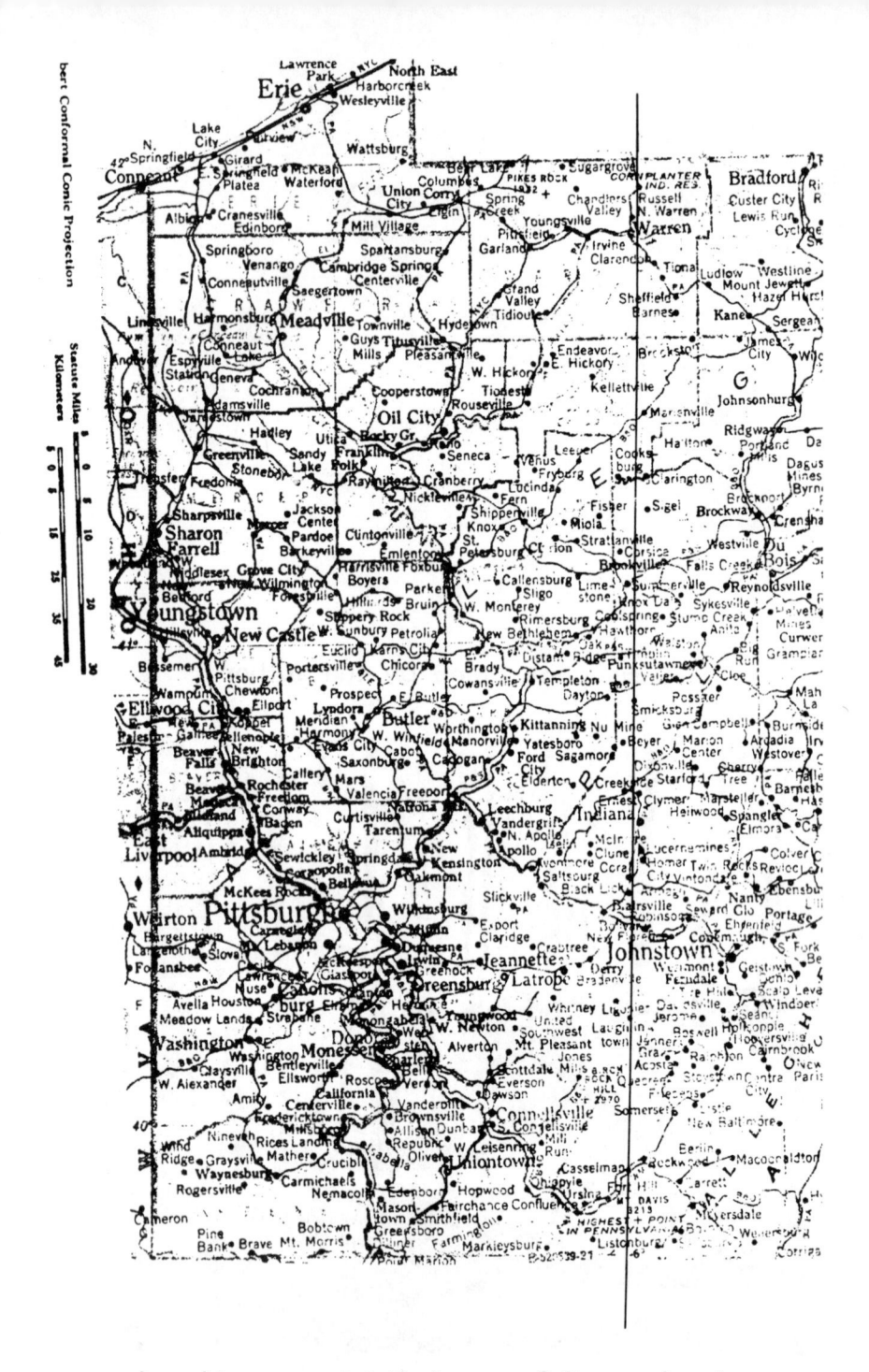

An old, more detailed map of Pennsylvania

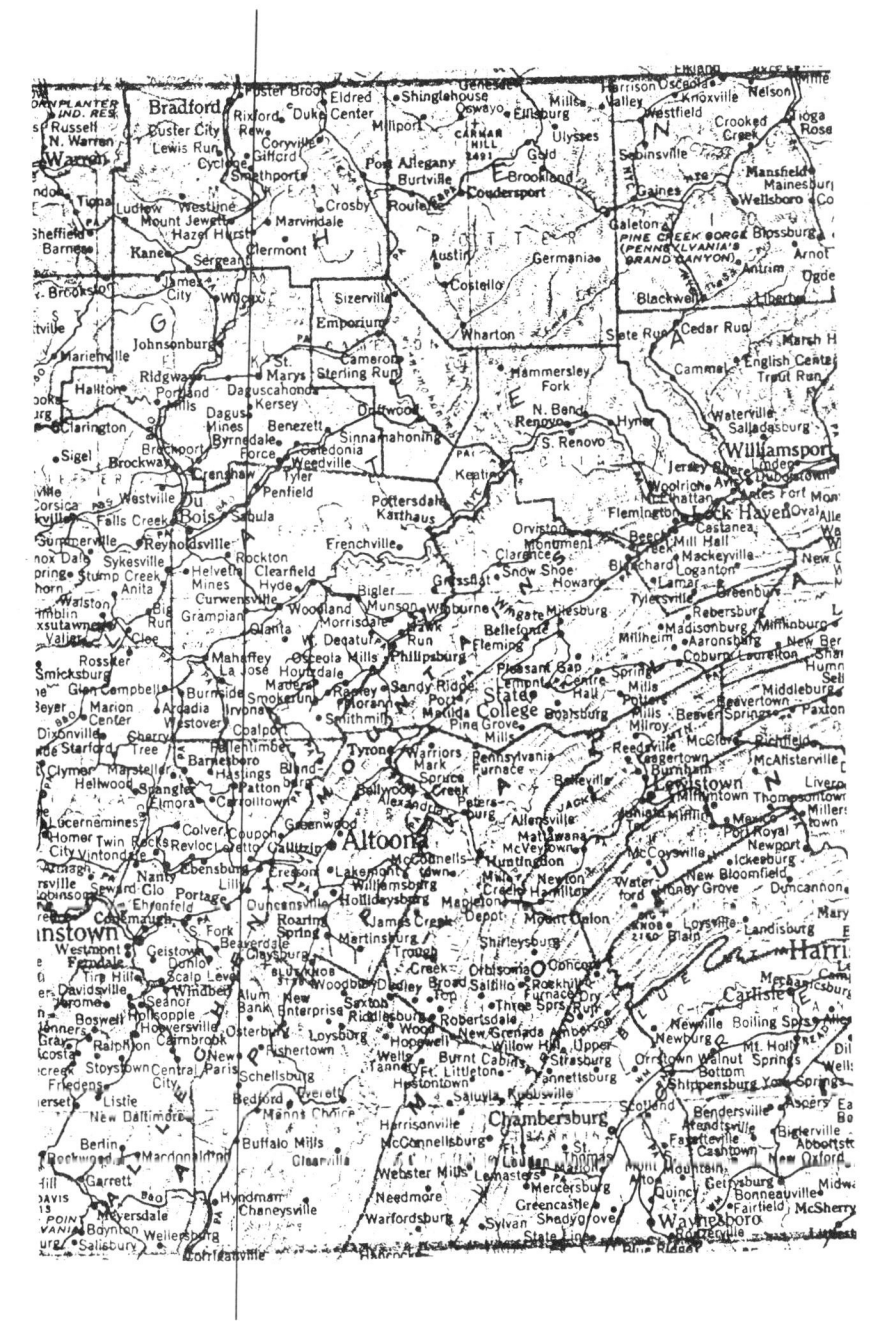

Maps on pages 104 and 105 overlap to the straight line top to bottom of the page

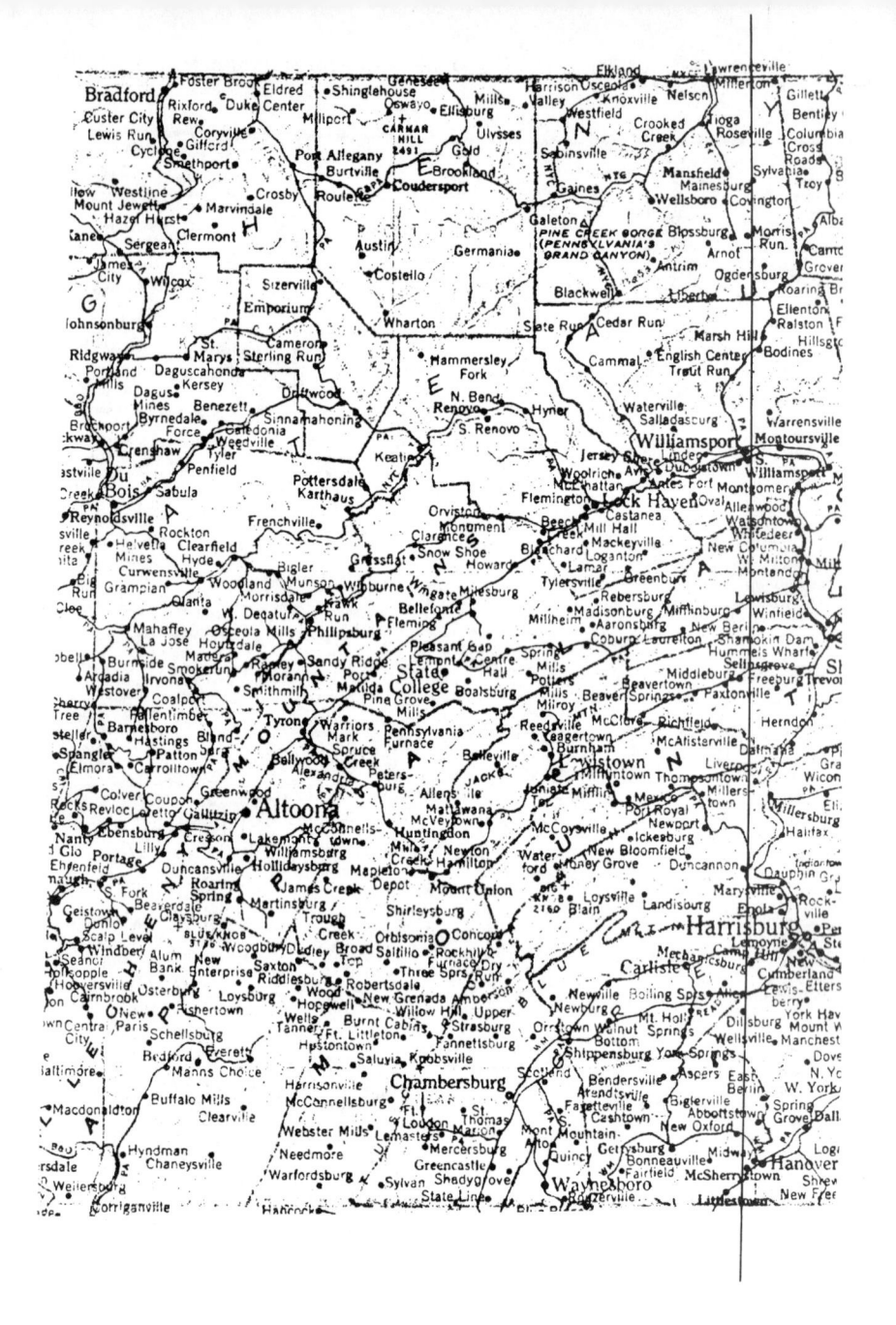

An old, more detailed map of Pennsylvania.

Maps on pages 106 and 107 overlap to the straight line top to bottom of the page.

Indian Signs can give you directions, tell a story or give a warning.